The
CORPORATE
EXODUS

How America's Top Companies
Build a Winning Culture
(to Attract, Keep and Develop their Emerging Leaders)

By Rae A. Majors-Wildman

The Corporate Exodus:
How America's Top Companies Build a Winning Culture
(to Attract, Keep, and Develop their Emerging Leaders)

Copyright © 2015 by Rae Majors-Wildman

ISBN 978-0-615-86110-4

First Edition

All the Way Success, Inc.
2604-B El Camino Real, Suite 182
Carlsbad, CA 92008

www.RaeMajorsWildman.com

Ordering Information:
Quantity sales. Special discounts are available on quantity purchases by corporations, associations, and others.

For bulk discounts or other
Corporate Culture Academy resources
Call 1-888-821-1822
email sales@raemajorswildman.com
or visit www.RaeMajorsWildman.com

Printed in the United States of America

This book is dedicated to my parents,
William and Carole Majors
Thank you for teaching me the
value of exceptional work ethics
and doing the right thing,
even when no one is looking.

Table of Contents

Chapter One

THE CORPORATE EXODUS

---

*"The growth and development of people
is the highest calling of leadership."
– Harvey S. Firestone, Founder of Firestone Tire and Rubber Company*

It was a beautiful Sunday morning, but Suzy stared out her window dreading the coming Monday. She had a ton of things on her desk that she left unfinished on Friday and thought about all of the meetings that were scheduled for this week. Oh, how she hated meetings. They were such a waste of time and it was just more of the same old things coming down from upper management—empty promises of things that the organization stated they would implement, only to leave undone once again. Tomorrow would be the day that she would finally depart from what she liked to affectionately call her "Golden Handcuffs." Her only fear was that she wouldn't have the courage to finally tell her boss that she's quitting.

This story is not unusual. As a matter of fact, the U.S. Department of Labor reports that between February 2012 and September 2014, an average of 2,000,000 people quit their jobs each month. How is it possible that so many people exodus from the corporate world, in hopes of creating a better life as an entrepreneur, even possible? What makes these individuals, who have exceptional salaries and benefits, decide that they'd rather risk it all and start their own business? Is it their desire to "be their own boss" or is it that they are just sick and tired of being an employee? The answer may surprise you, and this book is written to show you that there is a better way to run your organization and to challenge the old paradigm of "business as usual." If you embrace this new way of thinking, what is possible is mind-blowing and transformational, and your organization will never be the same.

In this book, you will learn the secrets from the top companies in the U.S. today. These companies are listed on *Forbes'* "Best Companies to Work For" and they not only attract the best talent in the world, they also have a different way of doing business—one that creates a culture with minimal turnover.

WHY I WROTE THIS BOOK

You may be wondering who I am, and what made me decide to become a reporter and compile this information. Let me share briefly that my journey started on the corporate path. I have worked for some amazing companies and I also had my own experience working with some companies that quite frankly were beyond terrible. However, when my son was six months old he was injured in day care, which forced me to make the difficult decision to quit my job and start my own company.

Entrepreneurship was never on my radar. As a matter of fact, I would consider myself an accidental entrepreneur. Today, I am the CEO of my own successful training and development company where I've had the great fortune of consulting and training some of the best entrepreneurs, small businesses, and Fortune 500 companies in the world. I also bring a fresh perspective as to why many great employees jumped ship and have decided to become the captain of their own vessel or work for the enemy *(also known as your competition)*.

One of the key things that I've learned after coaching and training thousands of people is that not *everyone* is cut out to be the boss. I know that might seem like a harsh statement, but the reality is that many people, if you really question them, don't want all of the responsibilities of running a successful company.

Think about it—you are actually a CEO, which means *Chief of Everything Officer*, and you are responsible for sales, marketing, finance, and operations. Not to mention giving up a steady paycheck and, of course, those coveted perks and benefits.

I've had the opportunity to ask these people what they really wanted when they started their businesses. For many people, it was a desire to make a difference, to feel appreciated and valued. I will talk more about that in the next section about why most employees quit. The truth is that, if they could have it their way, they wouldn't quit their jobs but would simply change the "culture" of their various workplaces.

This book is designed to give you and the leadership within your organization insights and strategies straight from America's top companies. You will learn how they align their values, mission, and purpose to create an empowering "winning" entrepreneurial culture. It is this culture that is the essence and the magnet for attracting top talent, creating change and innovation in the marketplace, and developing next generation leaders within their organizations. If you embrace and implement these strategies within your organization, you too will be able to attract amazing talent and you will absolutely change "business as usual."

If you are ready to create a world class business that you love, get ready, because it is actually possible and simpler than you can imagine! The first step on your journey is to understand what is making people jump ship.

WHY ARE THEY LEAVING?

There have been numerous debates as to the reasons why people leave their jobs. Many employers believe that it has to do with how much an individual earns. Although the ability of employees to take care of themselves and their families is important, it is not the primary reason why most people decide to escape the safety net to venture off on their own.

So why do they leave? Here are the top ten most common reasons why people quit their jobs:

1. Lack of Appreciation
2. Lack of Recognition
3. Lack of Growth/Advancement
4. Bad Management
5. Boredom
6. Poor Salary
7. Conflict with Fellow Co-workers
8. Work/Life Balance
9. No Accountability
10. Poor Communication

As you can see, money may have something to do with why some people quit their jobs. However, it is not the main reason why people look for greener pastures or decide to venture out to the uncertain world of entrepreneurship.

The popular Gallup polling organization surveyed over one million people to find out why employees did quit their jobs, and the number one answer was shocking. The reason why most people quit their jobs was not about them getting more money or promotions—the number one reason for most was simply that they didn't like their bosses. Let's look at the top ten reasons in more detail.

Lack of Appreciation

Everyone wants to feel appreciated and that their work is valuable. This is true both personally and professionally. Think about it. If you were married and every day your husband came home but never once told you that he loves you, that you matter to him, if he never thanks you for washing the dishes or taking out the trash, over time you will feel less warm and fuzzy about your relationship. The same is true of your employees. Saying thank you for a job well done goes a long way.

However, specificity is the key. It is not enough to just say thank you, according to Chester Elton, co-author of *The Carrot Principle*. When you can catch people doing a specific thing right and acknowledge them, they actually want to repeat the behavior and, more importantly, they feel like you care about them and that their role in the company makes a difference.

Lack of Recognition

Have you ever been in a meeting where you were brainstorming with other co-workers and you have a brilliant idea, only to find out later that someone else was given credit for your genius? As a leader of your company, the thing that will destroy trust quickly is failing to recognize the brilliance, talents, and gifts of your employees. Not only do employees feel like they are getting the shaft, it undermines the trust and respect which are essential ingredients for creating a winning culture. *(More about this later.)*

A key point to consider is that recognition can be both tangible and intangible. The question that many leaders ask is what the recognition should be. The best way to recognize your employees is to do something that would be especially meaningful to *them*. The more you know about your employees, the better you will become at recognizing and rewarding them for a job well done. A great example of getting to know your employees is demonstrated by Zappos. This online shoe company went from nearly bankrupt to generating over $1.2 billion in sales before being acquired by Amazon. Zappos' managers are encouraged to spend a minimum of 15% of their time with their direct subordinates doing *non-work* related activities. This is an excellent way for them to find out what

7

matters most to their employees. By doing so, you are able to recognize them in a way that makes them feel validated and appreciated.

Lack of Growth/Advancement

When hiring top talent, also known as superstars or rock stars, it is important that they are challenged and have an opportunity to grow. Many employers are afraid that they may be putting too much on their employees' plates, when in fact the opposite is true. Not having a clear blueprint on how to advance is one of the main reasons why your top talent will quit and go work for the competition. The problem that many companies face is when they are hyper-growing and are building the plane as they are flying, they are not quite sure what the next stage of advancement is for their employees.

It is important that you take the time to slow down, check in, and ask your employee where she sees herself in the next six months, one year, or five years within your organization. If she is uncertain about how to answer the question, I would suggest asking questions around the type of lifestyle she wishes to create outside of the job. The companies that are listed as "Best Places to Work" are notorious for having an educational budget for their staff. This benefit is to encourage employees to go back to school and attend personal development seminars or enrichment classes *(such as Spanish, Culinary Arts, and Coaching Certification)*. The key is to show your staff that growing is essential within the organization. By doing this, you will create an "intrapreneur" culture that will empower and foster goodwill, loyalty, and performance like you wouldn't believe.

Bad Management

Who is he or she married to? I can't tell you how many times I have worked for companies where you know without a doubt that the person in charge is only in charge because he or she is married to someone "at the top." Or is someone's child. Or [*fill in the blank*]. Don't get me wrong, I truly believe that as a business owner, you need to have a successor, and for many organizations it may be a spouse, child, or family member. But the problem with having bad management is that one bad apple truly does spoil the bunch. Leadership training is essential for anyone who is responsible for managing people and this is a great time to point out that just because someone is skilled at a task, such as sales, does not mean he would also be a great sales manager.

No one wants to work for someone who is an idiot. People want to know that the person in charge knows where the company is going and can chart the course for success. When people feel like the person in charge has no direction and no clue, they will decide to simply quit instead of having a "care-frontation"— especially if it seems as though their words will fall on deaf ears. In later chapters, I will share with you some examples of bad leadership styles.

Boredom

This goes back to employees' desires to grow and advance. There is nothing worse than waking up, driving to work, showing up and sitting at your desk, and doing the same monotonous task, day in and day out, especially if you are someone who loves a challenge. This is why it is so critical to have your employees take assessments, to be discussed in more detail when we talk about hiring the right fit. Just because someone is good at a task doesn't mean she should be doing it. What do I mean? In his book, *Go Put Your Strengths to Work* by Marcus Buckingham, the author shares the distinction between identifying your strengths and your weaknesses. How do you know the difference between a strength and weakness? Simply stated, if the task you are performing gives you more energy as you do it, then it is your strength. However, if the task drains or depletes your energy, then it is considered a weakness, even if you are great at doing it.

A practical example would be my ability to type 90 words per minute. I am a great and accurate typist, but I would rather have a root canal than spend eight hours a day doing data entry. I'm good at it, but it simply does not interest me. Do you have rock stars, superstars or "A" players in boring jobs? If so, you may want to consider moving them, or they will find themselves moving out.

Poor Salary

This goes without explanation. At the end of the day, people want to be compensated fairly for the work they do. I also want to reiterate the importance of making a difference and having a greater impact. If your organization is being built around the company's values and mission, and you have created a community of individuals who "buy in" to what the company or, more importantly, the leaders of the company believe, they are willing to take less pay if it means they are making a greater impact. They may even take a salary reduction in hard times to make sure that the company survives.

A great example of this is with a company named Barry-Wehmiller and their CEO Bob Chapman. During the recession, like many companies, there were difficult decisions that had to be made. Bob was faced with the decision to lay off people in order to help the company survive. However, Bob believes in Truly Human Leadership™ and he refused to lay off anyone. He challenged his leaders to come up with a solution where no one would be laid off. The answer was to create a mandatory unpaid furlough program where everyone from upper management to the front line would be required to take four weeks off without pay. This solution made it possible for everyone to keep their jobs, but the story gets better. The co-workers who had more financial resources opted to take more time so that others who were not in a position to do so could work. This is not something that was asked of them, they did it because that's what a true "winning" culture looks like and, by the way, that year they saved over $150 million in revenue and not one person was laid off. I love this story because it is a true example of how a great leader has the ability to empower, inspire, and rally the team together.

It is also important to note that, if you treat your people right, they will be loyal in return. Don't forget to reward them when you are reaping the fruits of their labor, and make sure you remember the sacrifices that they made. There is nothing more discouraging than to see a healthy increase in the profit margin and the only people who benefit are stakeholders and upper management. Money is not the main reason why people quit, but it is on the list nonetheless, so take care of your people and they will take care of you.

Conflict with Fellow Co-workers

We all have heard of the saying "going postal" and we know sadly of many incidents where an enraged co-worker shows up at work and does something that puts everyone at risk. According to the Census of Fatal Occupational Injuries *(CFOI)*, between 2006 and 2010 an average of 551 employees were killed as a result of work-related homicide. No one wants to be in an unsafe environment, and if you are working with individuals that you feel may snap or may be vocal and disrespectful, why stay in this type of environment? Does that mean that we are all going to get along every day and have no disagreements or differences in opinions? Of course not. We will have differences in opinion, and conflict will arise from time to time. It is the visionary's responsibility to clearly set the expectations and guiding principles for the company.

One of my favorite quotes goes something like this: "Conflict arises when expectations differ." Having conflict resolution processes in place will help you to navigate those situations when there are differences in expectations and opinions.

Work/Life Balance

This was the #1 reason why I became an accidental entrepreneur. When I gave birth to my youngest child, I had a strong desire to be home with my baby and the company that I worked for did not have flexible hours. They were unforgiving when I had to be home with a sick baby or when I wanted to go to the school play. That old paradigm of doing business is dead.

We are living in the global technology age when working 9 to 5 just doesn't work for everyone. In the book *The Work Revolution*, author Julie Clow describes how we were trained to work in the Industrial Revolution era and that allowing people to create their own schedules *(as long as the work gets done)* is not only productive, it also increases employee satisfaction and adds to the bottom line.

No Accountability

In a world where everyone does things their own way and it appears that no one wants to follow the rules, those who are successful know the importance of accountability. I have been coaching entrepreneurs, C-level executives, and small businesses for almost a decade and when I'm asked, "Why do most businesses hire you?" The answer is very simple. They want someone to synergize, brainstorm, and hold them accountable to the goals that they want to accomplish. Does this mean that these individuals are lazy or not driven? Far from it! These individuals are driven, goal-oriented, and focused, but they also know that, left to their own devices, they will find themselves succumbing to the urgencies and the fires of each day.

Many people quit their jobs because they wanted to be a part of the company's vision. They wanted to know exactly what the company's goals are, the target that the company is reaching towards, and their part in making it happen. They wanted to be kept in the loop and informed about what was happening within the organization. If you hold them accountable, they will flourish. However, if you simply have meeting after meeting with no clear action plan, you will find them running out the door.

Poor Communication

Communication is essential for building trust, respect, rapport, and a winning culture. Companies that excel at attracting and maintaining top talents are those leaders who inspire people through their communication skills. They are able to ignite and empower their teams to reach for higher heights, to believe the impossible, and to dominate their industry.

Apple's founder Steve Jobs was a powerful presenter, even though he was an introvert. He was brilliant at sharing what the vision of the company was and how he saw Apple as a brand. He has left a mark that will never be erased and it all began with his uttering these iconic words:

*Here's to the crazy ones, the misfits, the rebels,
the troublemakers, the round pegs in the square
holes...The ones who see things differently — they're
not fond of rules...You can quote them, disagree
with them, glorify or vilify them, but the only thing
you can't do is ignore them because they change
things...They push the human race forward,
and while some may see them as the crazy ones,
we see genius, because the ones who are crazy
enough to think that they can change the world,
are the ones who do.*

Remember, when it comes to communication, verbal communication is only 3% of what people hear. Conversely, 97% of all communication is made up of your body language, tonality, and what you *don't* say. As a leader, the first skill you must learn is to powerfully persuade and influence people, and this happens through your ability to communicate.

THE GENERATIONAL CHALLENGE ON THE HORIZON

This is the first time in our world's history that we will have four generations working in the workforce at the same time. Think about it...you have the Baby Boomers, Generation X, Generation Y *(also known as the Millennials)*, and Generation Z. Many companies are scrambling to determine how to leverage the wisdom of the Baby Boomers before they retire, and equip and empower the emerging leaders from Generations X, Y, and Z. As a leader, you must be able to communicate effectively with all generations, and if your company is to flourish and thrive you must understand what is important to each generation. One *size does* not fit all!

One other thing to mention is the increase of women in the workforce. One billion women were projected to enter the workforce from 2013 to 2022, and more and more women are demanding an opportunity to lead. The key to attracting and keeping top talent is to know what is important to them and how to make them feel valued. If you are unsuccessful, your organization will become a revolving door as your employees leave to go work for your competition, or they will seek to start their own companies and *become* your competition.

THE CORPORATE ESCAPE ARTIST

Now that we know the top ten reasons why people quit, it is no wonder that there are so many exiting the corporate world. I affectionately refer to them as "Corporate Escape Artists."

Who are these corporate escape artists? They are employees currently working at a company, while moonlighting or planning their escape to entrepreneurship. For many of these individuals, the entrepreneurial path makes perfect sense and might be the right career path for them. However, for the vast majority of individuals, the answer to finding career fulfillment is not breaking out of the corporate walls. Rather, it is simply leveraging their gifts, talents, and abilities with their desire to grow, make a difference, be challenged, and play a bigger part in the game.

If you can harness this passion for your company and empower these employees to become entrepreneurs *within* your organization, you will create a culture similar to those top companies that I had the unique honor to interview and research. These companies are listed on *Forbes* magazine's "Best Places to Work," and you know them well because they are doing things differently. Companies like Google, TRX, Facebook, Red Door Interactive, Zappos, Barry-Wehmiller, Infusionsoft, Qualcomm,

Intuit, and Southwest, just to name a few, are breaking the old paradigm, empowering their employees, aligning their values, and changing the world as we know it.

What's even more exciting is, you can use these same techniques, strategies, and philosophies to build a company where you are attracting top talent who are beating down your doors to be part of your organization. It all begins with YOU!

"Everyone wants to live on top of the mountain, but all the happiness and growth occurs while you're climbing it."

– Andy Rooney

Chapter Two

WHAT IS YOUR COMPANY CULTURE?

"The smartest business decision you can make is to **HIRE QUALIFIED PEOPLE.** *Bringing the right people on board saves you thousands, and your business will run smoothly and efficiently."*

– Brian Tracy (emphasis added)

When you enter the door of Google, it's as if you have entered the pages of *Alice in Wonderland*. From nap pods, to free food, to dry cleaners, Google has created a company that people are clamoring to become a part of. The question that many business owners ask is *What if I don't have a billion dollar company like Google or Facebook—how can I compete?* Culture is not about providing every benefit imaginable. Rather, it is more about how your employees feel about your organization.

Culture is defined by Webster's Dictionary as "the set of shared attitudes, values, goals, and practices that characterizes an institution or organization." Now that you know the definition of this powerful word, let's look at your company's culture and how you measure up with our nation's top businesses. Before you take the quiz, let me also share that every business has a company culture—either it was created intentionally or by default. The goal of your organization is obviously to have an *intentional* culture that is created and aligned with the values, attitudes, and practices of the leader*(s)*.

TRAITS OF A WINNING ENTREPRENEURIAL CULTURE

What makes a "winning entrepreneurial culture?" If we look at *Fortune* magazine, the list includes health care, child care, work/life balance, telecommuting, and unusual perks. Upon further investigation from other sources, including American Express' OPEN Forum, the list expands to include these specific categories:

- Leadership *(more importantly, authentic leadership)*
- Communications *(open door/no door policy)*
- Innovation
- Living the company's values and mission
- Employee empowerment and sense of autonomy
- Fostering a work environment of fun and creativity
- Flexible work schedules
- Commitment to personal growth
- Community spirit

- Great pay and incentives

Now let's look at some of the categories in more detail.

Authentic Leadership

Who wants to follow someone who is wearing a mask? Employees who can trust and respect their employer, leader, manager, or supervisor are more likely to be happier at their jobs. What I discovered from various interviews and research was the level of true admiration these employees had for their leaders. It doesn't mean that employees agreed 100% with everything that was being implemented. However, the winning culture had employees who respected their leaders' openness as well as their willingness to show their vulnerability.

Communication *(Open Door/No Door Policy)*

If you want to know the number one thing that will stop a company from growing fast and really dominating the marketplace, it is poor communication. The companies that we studied not only have an open door policy; many of them have a no door policy. What is a no door policy? A no door policy is when upper management is actually out on the floor with their employees and there are no offices. If you visit Zappos, you will find Tony Hsieh and other top executives' desks right in the middle of the office *(they affectionately call it "Monkeys' Row")*.

How can you tell if companies have an open line of communication? It is quite easy to identify. Take a visit to your company's lunch room, cafeteria, water cooler, coffee area, or employees' break room. What is the vibe when leadership walks in the room? Does everyone continue laughing and conversing, or do you find the room becomes so quiet that you can hear a pin drop?

What about your company meetings? Are your employees open to sharing their thoughts, whether good, bad, or indifferent? Great companies not only remove the barriers to open communication, they reward and encourage it via social media, intranet, company meetings, and other platforms.

Living the Company's Values and Mission

Having a mission statement, guiding principles, and values are great—but if no one knows what they are, what's the point? The companies that have raving fans as employees, vendors, and customers are the ones who know how to make their mission come to life, while making their core values actionable on a daily basis.

Fostering a Work Environment of Fun and Creativity

Many years ago I heard a great salesperson say to a prospect, "Life is too long to be doing something that you don't love." What a powerful statement, especially when most of us are thinking about how short our time on this earth is; imagine how long your time is when you are doing something that you hate. Companies like Southwest, Google, and Infusionsoft foster a work environment of fun and creativity. Foosball and ping pong tables, scooters that carry employees to meetings, or volleyball and basketball courts may seem like a waste of money, when in fact the opposite is true. Creating an environment where people can't wait to come to work, and they also hate to leave, generates huge dividends while increasing your profit margin.

Great Pay and Incentives

It is also important to note that companies who are ranked as "Best Places to Work" also are companies who value their employees enough to pay them well and incentivize them to do their jobs well. Receiving verbal recognition is nice, but if your employees are not making enough to pay for their living expenses, the praises will be short-lived.

These are just some examples of what the top companies are doing to create a winning culture. During later chapters, we will drill down and examine each of these categories and how you too can implement them, even on a small scale, to make a greater impact on your organization.

HOW DOES YOUR COMPANY MEASURE UP?

This book is designed to help the leadership of your organization to create a *winning entrepreneurial culture* to attract, retain, and develop your next generation of leaders *(or emerging leaders)*. Before you can change, you must know exactly where you are as a company. The first step to change is to assess what you are doing well, what specific things you need to improve on, and how to close the gap. When working with CEOs, executives, and leaders, the first thing we do is an assessment to see specifically what challenges the company may be experiencing.

Below you will find an assessment to help you identify what type of culture your company is currently operating out of. The questions are designed to be answered quickly—do not overthink your answers. The quiz should take approximately 6-8 minutes to complete. I would recommend that you go with your first instinct or reaction. Once completed, you will simply tally your points to learn the level where your company culture is currently residing. The key to getting an accurate assessment is for you to answer the questions honestly from where you are today, not from the past or where you foresee your company being in the future. You can also visit this website for additional resources: www.**TheCorporateExodusBook.com**.

TAKE THE QUIZ

Rate each statement using a scale from 1 to 5:

5 = Always

4 = Most Often

3 = Sometimes

2 = Rarely

1 = Non-existent

1) We have a systematic process for recognizing and appreciating our employees.

2) Our employees know our company values.

3) We have written a mission statement, guiding principles, and core values.

4) Our employees feel comfortable sharing their ideas.

5) We have an open door policy.

6) We have monthly meetings where employees are able to express their opinions.

7) Our employees have a documented career blueprint and know where they are going.

8) We have outside events to deepen relationships with employees.

9) We pay our employees well.

10) Innovation is an important part of our culture.

11) We have great benefits, including health care, day care, tuition reimbursement, etc.

12) We create ways for our employees to experience a healthy work/life balance.

13) Our company has an internal process to promote from within.

14) We have leadership training programs for our new managers or supervisors.

15) Our employees feel comfortable communicating breakdowns.

16) Our employees take responsibility and don't pass the buck.

17) Our method of leadership is based on fear and intimidation.

18) Are you afraid to share bad news with your employees?

19) At least some of our employees would volunteer to work for free if the company fell on hard times.

20) How quickly are ideas implemented?

Now add your scores for each question, and find your place on the Culture scale below.

Score of 21 - 40 = Level 1 Culture

Score of 41 - 60 = Level 2 Culture

Score of 61 - 80 = Level 3 Culture

Score of 81-100 = Level 4 Culture

Now that you know where your company culture currently stands, let's consider how you can make it better. The first step in transforming anything is to know where you are and where you want to go. If you are reading this book, it is my assumption that you want to create a *winning entrepreneurial culture* within your organization. Clarity is power, and we cannot improve that which we do not measure.

THE FOUR DOMINANT TYPES OF CULTURE

There are four types of culture that you will find within most organizations. In the book *Tribal Leadership*, the authors Dave

Logan, John King, and Halee Fischer-Wright discuss five "tribal stages" that many organizations may find themselves in. These stages really explain how individuals play in the proverbial sandbox together. To elaborate on their research, what I have discovered is that many companies' cultures can easily be found operating within one of the four cultures listed below.

Level 1 Culture: Just Give Me My Check

This is a culture where people literally just show up to do their jobs. The employees are dispassionate, disengaged, and do the bare minimum to avoid being fired. When asked to do something that is not in their job descriptions, they are the ones who complain, blame, and whine about not getting paid for doing a certain task. Normally this culture is the poster child for poor management, poor communication, and a survival mentality. This culture is difficult to change unless you literally remove the leader at the top.

I had the opportunity to do training at a particular company and during the goal-setting portion of the training I asked one of the senior managers to share his goals with the group. His answer was "I just show up every day and do my job. Other than that I don't have any goals." He is what some would call a short-timer. A short-timer is defined as someone who is counting down the days to retirement and has disengaged from the organization with no real desire to make any further contribution. Can you imagine what would happen if the company was able to ignite him by getting him to share his wisdom and mentor others before he walked out of the door? Indifference is a silent assassin in the Level 1 Culture.

Level 2 Culture: Management vs. Employees *(also known as "Them vs. Us")*

Have you ever worked for a company where you felt like you had to watch your back? It is as if your manager, leader, and/or boss are waiting for you to mess up so they can make an example out of you. In this environment, creativity and innovation is normally discouraged from employees. The leaders are the ones who have the "great" ideas and they do not welcome any collaboration from the staff. Mistakes and failures are looked upon as reasons for immediate dismissal and, because of this adversarial approach of leading, staff and leaders bond in a way that creates the culture of "Them vs. Us."

Also, you will notice that a Them vs. Us culture will reward the managers with bonuses and other special perks, while the staff and those on the front lines receive no additional compensation or acknowledgments for the work that they did to help their bosses to get that well-deserved bonus.

Level 3 Culture: Competing at Any Cost...Crabs in the Bucket, Rock Stars, Superstars, and Average Joes

In this culture, leadership fosters a sense of competition among the troops. There is favoritism and the rock stars/ superstars are rewarded, showcased, and praised, while others feel like they simply cannot compete. This ultimately creates a "crab in the bucket" attitude, or what the Australians like to call "tall poppy syndrome." Basically, you will find employees stabbing their fellow co-workers in the back to get ahead. In a Level 3 Culture, you may find rock stars or superstars are promoted to management positions because of their success in achieving company goals. The problem with these promotions is that many of these high-achieving employees do not have the proper leadership training to excel in their newly appointed positions. This ultimately creates an even more toxic environment and sense of resentment with the other employees.

Level 4 Culture: Together We Can Transform the World

This is what you would call Nirvana, or a *winning entrepreneurial culture*. In this culture, everyone is truly and sincerely focused on the mission and the greater good of the company. There is true collaboration, partnership, and a sense of family. The staff gets behind the leader and together they rise to compete, but not against each other *(or only in a friendly way)*. Instead, they compete against the greater evil— their competitors. This is the culture where people truly grow, challenge, and care about one another. It fosters a sense of family with your own particular language. It is what Seth Godin would call a "tribe." A tribe is defined as a group of people who are connected to each other, an idea, and a leader.

One of the best examples of a tribe is Apple. Not only have they created a tribe internally, their customers are a reflection of what a "Together WE Can Transform the World" culture looks like.

Now that you know the level of your company culture, we can begin helping you to work towards creating your ideal company culture. There are a couple of key points that you must consider in designing a winning culture. First, this is not a quick fix. It will take effort and time. It is also important to note that you cannot jump from Level 1 to Level 4 overnight. There is a process and you will find that you go from Level 1 to Level 2, so on and so forth. Also, once you reach Level 4, you have not arrived. The most important part of building a winning culture is in protecting and maintaining it. We will return to this in Chapter 7 when we discuss "Build It and They Will Come."

ENVIRONMENT TRUMPS WILLPOWER

As I mentioned earlier, your culture is being created either intentionally or by default. What is even more important to mention is "your environment always trumps your willpower." What is your environment? Simply stated, it is people, places, and things. It is the people that you hang out with, the places that you go, and the things that you own. If your employees are operating in clutter, their level of productivity will only go so far. If you have a Negative Nelly with enough influence in the group, that person will literally poison the environment and your culture.

A great example of this illustration was when I was shopping at my local Target store. That particular day, as I entered the checkout line there was a woman who was totally inspiring, she was so happy. She is what Mark Sanborn, author of *The Fred Factor* would call a "Fred." In his book, Mark defined a "Fred" as "someone who goes over and above the call of duty." Their level of customer service and enthusiasm is contagious. I must admit that I shop at Target at least once a week and I had never, in the nine years I lived in Southern California, experienced such joy and appreciation from any of their employees toward this company. She explained how much she loved her job and how it was such a great place to work. I left feeling pretty good about the company as well as this employee.

Two weeks later, I was back in the same store and as I was

walking around I overheard one employee telling the other how they couldn't wait to get off work in three minutes. In the grocery aisle, I heard another employee complaining about management and how they don't listen to their suggestions. In the beauty aisle, I heard an employee complaining about the flow team crew who was responsible for stocking the shelves, and how incompetent they were. And when I reached the checkout line, I saw the young lady from a couple of weeks before, and guess what she said to me? "This is the most boring job in the world. It is the same thing day in and day out." Let me say that I was disappointed, but not surprised. You may be asking what happened to the happy-go-lucky, joyful person who was so appreciative and excited about working for Target. It is simple—your environment will always trump your willpower.

It doesn't matter how positive you are. If you are hanging around with people who are negative, guess what? You will become negative as well. In future chapters, we will discuss how to protect your culture once created. I also want to point out that this is not an indictment of Target. You could substitute many other retail companies in the example. What I do know is that the experience made me want to contact their corporate offices and offer my services to them because this Level 1 Culture will not only impact their attracting the right employees, it will also keep customers from coming back.

In the next chapters, we will examine one of the most common yet valuable skills that those listed on Forbes' "Best Places to Work" exemplify. Master this skill and you will attract the right employees and customers that align with what you are all about.

"If everyone is moving forward together, then success takes care of itself."

– *Henry Ford*

Chapter Three

AUTHENTIC LEADERSHIP

---

*"To thine own self be true, and it must follow, as the
night the day, thou canst not then be false to any man."*
— *William Shakespeare*

AUTHENTICITY IS THE NEW LEADERSHIP CURRENCY

Authenticity and vulnerability seem to be the new buzz words within the business world. It is even more prevalent with the introduction of social media platforms such as Facebook, LinkedIn, Twitter, Pinterest, and Google+. In the past, CEOs, managers, and leaders would communicate only what they wanted their employees or customers to know—and what they didn't want them to know, they would simply keep hidden behind closed doors. However, with the invention of social media, many organizations find themselves being forced to become transparent, because there is no hiding when it comes to social media. That which is kept in the dark will eventually find its ways to the light.

Keep in mind that those companies who possess a winning entrepreneurial culture do not acquire it by accident; it is intentional, strategic, and by design. A winning entrepreneurial culture begins and ends with the CEO and leaders of the organization. If you examine any one of the top companies that we researched and interviewed you would noticed a common thread between these companies. Leadership is this common thread, but more importantly "authentic leadership."

A perfect example of a person who demonstrates authentic leadership is Sheryl Sandberg, COO of Facebook. In her book *Lean In*, she shares the challenges that she faced as a woman in business and the challenges that many women who are seeking to climb the corporate ladder face in regards to balancing their work and personal life. Sheryl's book was embraced by many; however, she also received some negative responses to her viewpoint.

Being an authentic leader is not about making everyone happy. It is about showing up without the mask and sharing how you feel openly, with vulnerability and integrity. It is about being real. It is about showing up and saying, "This is who I am" and when you share your experiences, both successes and failures, your authenticity becomes magnetic. True authenticity as I have described it will attract or repel your ideal customers, vendors, and employees.

Another example of an authentic leader is Gary Vaynerchuk, who started Wine Library TV and is now CEO and co-owner of VaynerMedia. This New Jersey native is loud, boisterous, and has a knack for telling it like it is, and his personality is such that you either love him or hate him. There is no middle ground. That is the power of authenticity. When you are your authentic self, it becomes very easy to find your tribe and to build your culture, because when you are doing this, besides just being you, people will resonate with you and they will want to come on the journey and be part of what you are doing.

TRUST PROCEEDS RESPECT

Employees are looking for the leader to be open and honest with them. According to a study conducted by the *Harvard Business Review* and Tony Schwartz, when it comes to garnering commitment and engagement from employees, there is one thing that leaders need to demonstrate—respect. Employees who got respect from their leaders reported 56% better health and well-being, 1.72 times more trust and safety, 89% greater enjoyment and satisfaction with their jobs, 92% greater focus and prioritization, and 1.26 times more meaning and significance. Those who felt respected by their leaders were also 1.1 times more likely to stay with their organizations than those who didn't.

What most employers do not realize is that employees are generally tougher than you give them credit for. How do you share bad news with your employees? *Do* you share bad news with your employees? Many leaders question what they should or should not share with staff. They fear that if they let them know things are not going as well as they should, they may find themselves losing great employees.

The reality is that when you do not communicate with your staff it actually causes them to speculate, which is never good. I have coached hundreds of business owners, and I have watched them worry themselves sick about how they are going to take their business to the next level or how they are going to pay their bills. It is a great weight to bear as CEO of a privately held organization. However, when you open up and let the right people in, you will experience a business like no other.

During my interviews and research, I had the opportunity to speak to quite a few employees and many of them shared how their CEOs, founders, or presidents were infectious with their vision. They also shared that they joined the organization because they wanted to be part of something bigger than themselves. And what is also worth mentioning is how they appreciated the CEOs' transparency.

In the case of TRX Training, founded by Randy Hetrick, what inspires his employees to give 110% comes down to his ability to innovate a somewhat stagnant industry. When the company first started, one of the things that was implemented was "All Company" weekly meetings, where the employees were basically given a scoreboard of what was going on within the company. Randy's willingness to share the company's numbers with his employees may be considered as risky. However, when you are building a winning entrepreneurial culture, it is essential that you have your employees buy in, and that only happens by coming together as a team and sharing what is truly going on. In later chapters, we will share how to do this in a way that will empower the organization, and how by doing so, you create a Level 4 Culture that will do whatever it takes to win.

Every company meets challenges on the way to becoming a success. Many of the companies that we interviewed were on the verge of closing their doors and many have faced disastrous setbacks. Whether it's Apple CEO and founder Steve Jobs, who was fired from the company that he created, or Tony Hsieh who had to bring the startup Zappos into his physical home—literally—every leader will experience up and downs. What makes them true leaders is their ability to openly share with those who are on the journey with them what is going on.

Another thing I have learned is that many leaders want to be respected by those they lead, but fail to realize that it all starts with trust. It begins with the leader building trust first, and then respect will follow. How do you build trust with your employees? It starts with walking your talk and doing what you say you are going to do. Trust is only built over time through repetition and frequency. Trust happens when you allow yourself to show your vulnerability and authenticity. Trust also is developed through consistent communications.

I cannot express this enough! I have worked with some top level companies *(who will remain nameless)*, and the breakdowns they were experiencing were not because of the market, lack of innovation, or their competition. The breakdowns happened internally when the employees heard the news about being acquired over the Internet, newspaper, or TV. How would you feel if you went home and were told by your spouse that your company was sold, and you didn't have a clue? Exactly!

Building trust with your employees can be as simple as having weekly or monthly meetings to share what's going on, or even sending out monthly email communications. Let me just say that if the news is something that is serious, it is important that you take the time to share with the staff in person if possible or, at a bare minimum, to communicate via conference call.

TAKING OFF THE MASK

It is when you realize that you do not have to be perfect that you are able to take off the mask and stop hiding your faults and weaknesses. It is when you allow your team to know that you need them and that the calling, mission, and vision for the company are bigger than you. And that it is impossible for you to bring it into the world without their support. Taking off the mask is scary; however, when you hire the right people, you realize that they will not let you fall, they are all in, and they are 100% behind you.

I recall talking with a business owner whose company was on the verge of bankruptcy. They had been in business for over ten years and when the recession hit, they found themselves barely able to keep their doors open. They had exhausted every resource; they had maxed out their lines of credit and were waiting for their proverbial *ship to come in*. During this trying time, this company had an opportunity to bid on a huge contract that would literally turn everything around if they won the bid. However, time was running out. They couldn't pay their vendors, bill collectors were calling them all hours of the day and night demanding them to pay their invoices, and I remember the CEO sharing that his lowest moments were when he realized that he was not going to be able to make payroll.

Left with no options, this brave entrepreneur decided that he needed to let his employees know that he would be closing the doors and that he valued their services. And if they needed a reference letter, he would be more than happy to give them one. The employer called the important "All Company" meeting and he shared what they had been experiencing for the past several months. In shame, he explained that he would not be able to pay them their salaries, and how sorry he was that he was not able to turn it around.

What happened next would literally give you goose-bumps as it did me when he shared his story. The employees told the CEO emphatically that he couldn't quit and throw in the towel. The employees all stated that they would work for FREE until the contract came through. Here's where it gets even more inspiring. These same employees raised money and gave it to their boss so that he could pay his mortgage along with other additional expenses. You see, they were grateful because he had been good to them for the past ten years. It was more than a job to them, they were family. This is a perfect example of a Level 4 Culture.

Happily, the contract was awarded to this amazing company and they were able to turn it around. How many of your employees would volunteer to work for free? How many of your employees have your back? This is a true example of a powerful and winning entrepreneurial culture. When you create a dynamic culture, there is a sense of trust, respect, and "all in" together mentality. However, the employer would have never experienced such a massive breakthrough and support if he had not been authentic, vulnerable, and transparent. When you have the right people on the team, they will do whatever is necessary to reach the company's mission.

IMPERFECTION AND EXCELLENCE

Many leaders struggle with a need to be right, or they struggle with perfectionism. On the surface, you may be wondering what is wrong with wanting things done perfectly. There are several reasons why perfectionism actual stalls the growth of an organization. Have you ever worked for a company where you presented ideas, only to find out that you had to go through a boatload of red tape to get your idea implemented?

Let's look at our government, whether the local, state, or national level. Many government officials struggle to make a great change or any real difference, solely because of the amount of bureaucracy within the government sector. This is the same struggle you will often see within the business sector.

This is why many Level 1 or Level 2 Cultures never seem to advance. With that said, I believe that it is important as a leader that you embrace a spirit of excellence over perfection. One of my former employers, Brian Buffini, CEO of one of the top real estate training companies, defined excellence as:

"Doing the best that you can, with the information that you have, in the time frame allowed."

Let's examine this philosophy further:

"Doing the Best That You Can...

When you are working on introducing a new project, launching a new product or service, or creating a new system or process within your organization, it is important that you gauge your success by the above statement.

Are you doing the best that you can? This does not mean that you are doing everything perfectly. As a matter of fact, I heard an entrepreneur once describe building a business like *building a plane while flying.* This is an excellent metaphor for any organization who desires to build a winning entrepreneurial culture. It truly is about your building the plane as you are flying it.

And when you answer the question, "Is this the best that I can do?" you will give yourself the grace to be able to launch without everything being done perfectly. When we look at innovation in future chapters, you will understand this concept further.

Perfectionism is the *mother* of procrastination. Remember that *done* is better than perfect. Let go of the desire to be perfect and embrace doing the best that you can...

...*With the Information that You Have*...

The other key point of working from a place of excellence is looking at the current resources that you have available to you. When you are launching a product, what are the key critical ingredients that you need in order to have a successful launch? Who are the key players who can add additional value to your project, program, or services? Excellence requires that you seek out as much information as you can without being paralyzed with the desire to know more.

There is a great AT&T commercial, where there is a man interviewing some very bright, young elementary school children. One of the questions that he posed to the group is, "What is better? Is it better to have more?" The children's response is, "More is better!" Well in this example, more information can be a hindrance. I see many businesses that are always researching, gathering data, and creating spreadsheets, but they never push the launch button. They are always getting ready to get ready, and they miss the opportunity to be the first in the industry to introduce a new innovation.

At some point, you have to take what you have and be okay with launching, knowing there is still more you could do. Why do you think we have Microsoft Windows Version 8 or iPhone 6? It is simply because they are providing the best product with the information that they have...

...*In the Time Frame Allowed"*

When you think about technology and innovation, speed is critical. Many businesses in that space find themselves chasing after the revolutionary company that brought the technology to market. The last thing you want to do is chase the competition. For many businesses, what you will learn is that your tribe will pay you to get it right.

The early adopters want to be the first to try out the new technology and they are okay that it's not perfect. As a matter fact, we have been conditioned that this new product is just temporary. No one purchases a phone or a computer with the expectation of keeping it for more than two years. Why? It is because we know that there are always newer technology and advances that are happening every day and we will continue to buy the best now, in hopes for better later.

That is why it is so important to allow yourself to provide excellence knowing that you will be able to create a better version later. How your product or service gets better comes down to the feedback you will receive from the marketplace, focus groups, and your employees. It requires that you launch and ask for the community to support you in creating something great.

If you look at those companies on the "Best Places to Work" list, you will discover this is the exact mindset that they have when launching new products or services. Speed is essential when it comes to technology and innovation. It is important as an authentic leader that you focus on excellence, not perfection.

"Perfect is the ENEMY to done." – Rachel Skylar

BRINGING IT ALIVE

Now is the time for you to roll up your sleeves and take a deeper dive with this content. My hope is that you are reading this because you have a desire to change your organization. Remember, it starts and ends with the leader. After each chapter you will be presented with a challenge that will drill deeper into the *Align* system. This is the foundational work that I am hired by organizations like yours to come in, assess, and coach them on.

The first step is to be open and honest. By truly sharing what is going on in your organization, you will be able to make the necessary changes to go from a Level 1 Culture to a Level 4 Culture. This is also an excellent exercise to have your key team members go through as well.

Let's go...

BRING IT ALIVE: ALIGNMENT CHALLENGE 1

Step One: Authentic Leadership

1. How do you define authentic leadership?

   _____

   _____

2. List examples within your personal and/or professional life where you have demonstrated authentic leadership.

   _____

   _____

3. From a scale of 1 to 10 *(10 meaning totally, 1 meaning suspicious)*, how much does your team trust you? What could you implement within your organization that would foster and increase trust?

   _____

   _____

4. Do you currently feel like you are wearing a mask? How has wearing this mask protected you?

   _____

   _____

5. Do you struggle with perfectionism? Share an example where you implemented without having everything prepared perfectly. What was the result of your taking this action?

   _____

   _____

New Business Culture Revealed: Case Study of "Best Places to Work"— Zappos

RMW: So I've heard quite a bit about your four-week new hire training and Zappos' commitment to culture. The question that I have is, how do you hire the right fit? When I look at your wall of fame and going from $1 million dollar day to $12 million dollar day, obviously there is a lot of growth in that. How do you hire fast and maintain your winning culture?

Zappos: A lot of it starts with the core values. And the fact that we quantify and say out loud what our culture means to us. The ten core values we have are all actionable. *(i.e. delivering wow through service, embrace and drive change, create fun and weirdness, etc. They are all verbs and the behaviors that go with each.)* For instance, when delivering wow through service, one of the behaviors is consistently going over and beyond what is expected. To create fun and a little weirdness means expressing yourself, expressing your true personality at work—not having a different persona. So, when it comes down to recruiting and hiring, we look for those behaviors throughout the interview process.

RMW: And how long is the interview process?

Zappos: It depends on the position. If it is a CLT position, Customer Service position, we typically get those filled in weeks. We open them up in small parts because we have the new hire training classes monthly. So those typically are 3-5 weeks from beginning to end. If it's a developer, senior level developer, or software engineer, it could take 6 months to a year. Our goal from a recruiting standpoint is whether it took six months to fill this position last time. This time we want to fill it faster, of course, but we always want to make sure that culture and technical fit are equally matched. So, if someone is a great technical fit but we do not feel they are a great culture fit, we will pass.

RMW: I heard that one of the steps in your interview process is for the interviewee to submit a video.

Zappos: Yes, we encourage video submission but we don't require it. We also encourage people to submit creative cover letters. Cover letter videos are the ones we see most often and that's because pretty much everyone can create a cover letter video—it just requires a video cam and it doesn't take anything fancy. One of the coolest ones that I got was a resume on a bottle of wine. And I'm not even a recruiter. It was pretty cool, I have it sitting at home and I won't open it. She currently works for a wine distributor in Chicago and she sent a bottle of wine.

RMW: That's awesome. So what I heard you say is making sure the culture and the technical fit is the first priority. How do you protect the culture?

Zappos: A lot of it does start in recruiting. After they submit a video cover and resume we will do a phone screen. The phone screen is to discover the prospect's personality, for example "Can you talk to someone?" Then the process is pretty rigorous. After the phone screen the next step would be a Skype interview or a video interview which instead of Skype in real time, it is actually sending people a list of questions and asking them to answer the questions on video. It is uncomfortable and we are not looking for people to be the next Jane Pauley or Matt Lauer, but we want to kind of see who you are when you answer the questions. At that point, we move on to the next round, and bring them in for an in-person interview. If they are local it's easy; if they are not local, we usually narrow it down to 5 candidates before we start flying people in. When they come in…

RMW: Do they fly in on their dime?

Zappos: No, we will pay for them to fly in. When they come in *(if they are from out of town)* we do it all at one time, like a blitz.

It's a long day. It's testing. Everyone has the same testing—it's Internet skills test, a little bit of data entry, can you take orders on the site, typing, and grammar. No matter who you are, you have to pass the test and also we are paying attention to things like what's your attitude when you're testing. If someone said, "I can't believe you are having me take a typing test," or "Yeah, I can write this site," that's a red flag to us. We're not going to send you home that morning but you probably are not going to be hired. By the same token, those things seldom happen. That's kind of what I like about the Skype interviews—we are kind of getting a feel for them before they show up. They will have testing and if they are up for a technical position, they will have an interview with the technical hiring manager, culture interview with the recruiter, and also at this point we will add a team interview. This is basically to evaluate team fit. Lunch maybe...then go out for drinks later. More relaxing, this is just to see how they fit in with the team and if personalities mesh.

The Skype interview also includes technical components and culture. Culture is always by the recruiter, technical by the hiring manager because he or she knows what is needed for the position. Once we have done all those rounds of interviews, we will compile feedback. Everyone will give feedback. Ultimately the hiring manager and the recruiter will make the decision together. Again the recruiter is there to be the guardian of the culture and I don't mean it's adversarial at all; it's just that if you have a spot to fill on your team yesterday, you're not likely to see things that a recruiter is there to see.

RMW: It's more the checks and balances.

Zappos: Exactly! Exactly! It really, really helps and the recruiters are really skilled at asking questions that draw people out. Like a question would be, "Tell me about a time you were part of a team working on a project and things didn't go the way you planned?" And it's very open ended and the recruiters are skilled at assessing the little things.

RMW: They are in the initial interview process. They are the ones that are protecting the culture.

Zappos: Exactly. That's for the initial process and then afterwards when they join our family, it becomes everyone's job to protect the culture.

RMW: Now that's the piece I'm intrigued about. How does everyone protect the culture?

Zappos: Now that comes with training, which is the second part of what you asked. The four weeks of onboarding which everyone is going through is half-technical aspect of customer service. Everyone goes through it—CFOs, Tony's gone through it. The reason is, customer service is not a department—it is who we are as a company. Our first core value is deliver wow through service. Our mission statement is to live and deliver wow experiences. We believe that customer service is number one and everyone has a customer. You're my customer right now. If I am in HR or I'm a recruiter, my customer is everyone who applies for the position. If I'm HR, every employee is my customer. And we want to make sure that we are giving them a good service experience from the time they apply to the time they leave here for the last time, even if we are exiting someone. We want to make sure that we do it with service and with that in mind.

And so tackling the service aspect in new hire training and onboarding really helps. It helps us with other things because everyone does help out on the phones during the holidays. The Zappos way of doing customer service is within the context of answering the phone. The other half of the four weeks of the onboarding is culture training and immersion. Most people see our culture, they come and take tours, and they say oh, it is fun, but there are reasons why we do what we do. And it gives them an opportunity to see it firsthand. The first week is a presentation, which is the history of our values. We haven't always had our core values—they were rolled out in 2006.

RMW: And who created them?

Zappos: Actually it was input from everyone from the company at the time. Tony sent an email out to the entire company back in 2005 asking them a couple of questions. One of them was, "What are your personal values?" And "What do you really value in life?" And the other one, which was really telling, was "Look around at your co-workers and who do you see that actually embodies Zappos?" Then, "Who do you think is the ideal person to represent Zappos and what are the behaviors that person exhibits?" Which is how we ended up with something that was actionable. The answers started rolling in and we ended up with a list of 37 characteristics, traits, and behaviors. Then a smaller group of people *(about a dozen or so)* worked to concentrate them down to the 10 core values that we now have. Because thirty-seven is quite a lot.

The core values actually provide structure. I kind of think of them as the scaffolding for our culture. It is very deliberate and intentional on a macro scale, so that on a micro scale, things can happen naturally and it's because there is that existing support. Some of the things we do are definitely engineered. In this building we only have one exit that's not an emergency exit, and one entrance. That's so we are all coming in and we see other. I see people in the lobby that I haven't seen for months. Tony refers to them as serendipitous interaction but is it forced that I bumped into someone in the lobby at that time? But the environment is created so that it can happen and so that those things can thrive. The team structures are really helpful. We ask our managers to spend 10-15% of their time with their employees not doing work related things.

We call them a one-on-one. Or maybe it's not. Maybe you are going to have coffee across the street. Or we will go to the movies together and do things like that. We encourage people to spend time with each other away from work. Not saying that you have to go to every happy hour that you have to spend 6 hours a week with your employees outside of your 40. A lot of it is built right into the work day. But getting away from the daily tasks to know each other, because the more you get to know each other the better you will work with each other.

RMW: If you have someone who happens to slip through Zappos, and it happens... where they might be brilliant at their skill set but they may not be a fit, are they given a performance plan?

Zappos: Yes, we will give feedback. Because their behaviors are tied to the core values and because those behaviors are an expectation for employment. We can give feedback on those behaviors and give those people a chance to improve. In general, people are not jerks. They might just have jerky tendencies that we don't even realize until someone brings it to our attention.

RMW: So that's the accountability piece. They are being held accountable.

Zappos: Absolutely. Our annual reviews, the only annual review that everyone gets that is actually the same, is actually culture based. It's 30 questions right now, I heard a rumor that the new review will have 50 and they are questions about behavior. Out of ten times, how many times have you observed Kelly accepting that good ideas can come from anyone? How many times out of ten have you observed Kelly being willing to push on and not take no for an answer? Those are the behaviors and those become the expectation of your job performance in addition to whatever other metrics you are held to. And we give people feedback if necessary and there is not any improvement. In addition to the feedback, we will work with you and say, what can we do to help you with this? Is there someone you really look up to that seems to embody this particular behavior, and would you like to shadow that person? Whatever it is to get that employee to that level, and we work from there. And if we need to we will...

RMW: Reintroduce them back into the marketplace.

Zappos: That's right. We will promote them to customer. And it's okay. Everyone is not a fit all of the time, but that doesn't mean the person is a jerk. It's just not a right fit for them or us.

RMW: I'm curious about Amazon acquiring Zappos in 2009. How has that impacted the culture, if any or not at all?

Zappos: At first I will be very honest, we were all a little worried who were here. What's kind of funny is now more than half of the employees who work here have been here less than two years because of our growth. Most of the company does not remember a pre-Amazon time. Which is weird and it also means that we have to be very intentional about telling our story because we are growing so fast. We have to let new employees know our history and what it took to get us here. We didn't always have matching 401k plans and a gym and a coffee shop. We didn't always have those things and it's really easy to take them for granted. Holy smoke, it is easy to take them for granted but by telling those stories and reminding each other and ourselves that hey, this is a cool thing that we have, it helps with that kind of entitlement. Which is one of the things a lot of companies battle and it's a struggle for us. Scaling the culture and battling entitlement are the two biggest challenges.

As far as the changes from Amazon, a lot of it has been systematic, like our warehouse management system had to change. We handed over warehouse operations to Amazon which has been the biggest change for us, to date. It was hard, but we recognize that it's best for our customers because Amazon is really good at cheap, fast fulfillment. We are good at fast fulfillment but not necessarily cheap, fast fulfillment. They are more efficient at it. It is also better for the warehouse employees because they are around a company that is designed around fulfillment so they have an idea what it takes to grow those employees, whereas for us we are kind of jacks of all trades in that. It wasn't our core competency, so that would be the biggest change. Culturally it really hasn't affected us. In fact, in many ways it's kind of helped us, because Amazon is committed to helping us be us. We are a wholly owned Amazon company but we operate independently from them. So really the difference is, Tony goes to Seattle and reports to the Amazon board every quarter.

RMW: Do you see Tony here regularly?

Zappos: Yes, he's here at the office or at the Carson office. I see him probably 4 or 5 times a week and I'm not even in this building. He takes a lot of meetings downtown because he lives downtown and he's splitting his time between Zappos and DowntownProject.com and probably it's not a 50/50 split because at Zappos he has things in place so it can run without him.

RMW: If Tony stopped showing up to work today, the company is self-sufficient and will still exist.

Zappos: Exactly. And Downtown Project, since it's new, it still needs him a lot. Whereas Zappos is Zappos. Downtown Project is very closely associated with Tony.

RMW: How do you hold your employees accountable?

Zappos: Yes, it is through the coaching and behaviors. We also encourage our employees to fill out an assessment for their supervisors. It's different from department to department but it can become part of my managers' assessment/review. Not all managers are there yet with their teams, but we are lucky because we are relatively a small team, and because we are training, we are used to giving and receiving feedback all the time. We are a lot more comfortable with it, even by Zappos' standards. But the other thing is everyone has a "Skip Meeting" which could be quarterly or monthly depending on the supervisor. Ours are quarterly because my manager's manager has 100 people that she has to meet with. But basically we go to lunch with my manager's manager *(I skip my manager)* and she actively asks questions, for instance "How do you feel about this within your team?" to gather feedback for our managers, and it's informal. We usually do it in groups of three or four but you can do one-on-one if you'd rather, it's entirely up to you. I trust my team, I have no problem giving feedback and the other thing for me is I'm very fortunate that I have a close relationship with my manager, so there's nothing that I'm going to tell her manager that she hasn't heard from me first.

RMW: It's that open dialog.

Zappos: Yes. That is really important. It's that sense of trust. Not everyone has that and recognizes that, and that is one of things that we are working on with our leadership program. As we build out classes for our leadership program to give managers tools, concrete things that they can take with them so they can build that trust. With people only being here for two years or less they come in with a lot of baggage from other jobs. I had some great jobs with some terrible bosses in the past and we all kind of bring that in here with us.

RMW: It's like drinking the Kool-Aid.

Zappos: It is like drinking the Kool-Aid. We call it alignment.

RMW: That's part of the book…it's about aligning your core values to build a winning culture.

Zappos: Yes, and I think it's important for any company to state their core values. I feel like, if I'd been around Zappos and never heard the core values, that when I heard the core values I would be able to say oh yeah, that makes sense. I see that. Our core values are who we are when we are at our best self. And we actually miss the mark from time to time because we are far from perfect, but that is what we are striving for. So for me as an employee or a recruit I want to look at them and say yes, I'm aligned to that. They don't have to be the exact same, but nothing in my personal values conflicts with those values or you won't be happy and you won't be successful.

RMW: I truly believe that. What would you say the secret sauce for this company is?

Zappos: I think it really comes down to trust and empowerment. Trusting your employees to make the best decisions and empowering them to make those decisions. We still have checks and balances in place, especially when it comes to certain things. We have to be PCI compliant because we take credit cards. We are part of a publicly traded company so there is SEC stuff. We have all of those things but the fact remains that as a company, as an employee, I am given certain things that are my scope of work and I am charged with doing what it takes to get that job done. And if I get stuck and I hit an obstacle. I have resources I can access—either co-workers or managers or someone along those lines—to help me remove those obstacles or get over them. But the fact remains I don't have to go and check every little decision, and that is on the floor with our front line employees, in our facilities teams, it's something that we want *(people making the decisions)*, which is why the hiring process is pretty rigorous, the training process is four weeks, because once you get out of that you are pretty much kind of set free, too. So we want to make sure we got the right fit and you are going to make the right judgment. You get on the phone and people can give away free product if necessary. We do ask that they use good judgment, if it's a $15 pair of socks maybe a $5,000 coupon is not an appropriate response. If we have employees who do that we can address that situation. We have a policy here at Zappos that we don't make rules for the exception. If this comes up we will address it and we will move on from there. It's a learning experience for the employee and for the person giving the feedback and everything is hunky dory.

RMW: Is there a career path for your employees?

Zappos: Yes. It depends on the department. Merchandising and TLC have a lot of people. A supervisor will have 2-4 teams, managers, directors, senior directors. You can come in as a buyer, lead buyer, and you will have a certain career track. When it comes to smaller departments, we have cross-training and our progression is a little different. Our overall annual turn is about 20%, 16% will leave the company where

4% will transfer to other departments for promotions or growth opportunities.

RMW: Will you hire internally first?

Zappos: Yes, we will always hire internally first and then we will look outside if we didn't get any nibbles.

RMW: What would you say that you would love to see change, if anything?

Zappos: Gosh. If I had a magic wand I think that as we grow, my magic wand would be to see …as I mentioned that entitlement is sometimes an issue. I would like to see as a company to not be so generous with employees. I just found out today that they sell bus passes here. I asked, how much is the bus pass? The bus pass at Zappos is $10. The actual bus pass is $65, so Zappos is underwriting $55/month, and I looked at it and I said you kidding right One of the guys standing there from Finance said "I know, right?" As an employee, I would love to see us contribute a little more. He said, as someone in treasury, so would he. Sometimes I feel like as a company we are too generous and maybe people need a little bit of a reminder. And we do seem as a company not to talk about bad stuff. Maybe it's my age…

RMW: What's the average demographic of your employees?

Zappos: The average age is thirty-five. But it seems like a lot younger. And sometimes it really bugs me. We have a joke and we will say what if we do a day without culture? And my response is, "Hey guys, there's no Bistro today, or Bistro is $10."

RMW: Like a reality check. You can call it "Reality Friday"

Zappos: We do work in smaller ways. We check each other on it. There have been days when I've been in the lunchroom and hear these words come out of my mouth and wonder where they come from, "There's no chocolate ice cream here today?" And then my friend will look at me and say "Did you just say..." Yeah...thanks for calling me on it.

RMW: How do keep entitlement from creeping in?

Zappos: It's tough. It can creep into all of us but it's really hard and that's part of our jobs when we are hiring people is telling the stories, telling them about our history and reminding them that it is pretty cool what we have and we are grateful and we work really hard. I think that's a misconception about people who join us—they see the "Play Hard" and the reason we play hard and the reason we have a lot of these on-site services is because management recognizes that we work really hard and so let's make life a little easier where we can. Let's face it ...they may lose money on the employees lunch but they also gain productivity time. Because I'm spending my lunch hour going somewhere and I actually get to enjoy my lunch hour then I come back refreshed and can dive right in to whatever project I was working on.

RMW: Not only that, you also get to connect with your co-workers and you're deepening and building the culture.

Zappos: Exactly.

RMW: What would be the one thing you would want my readers to know about Zappos?

Zappos: I think a lot of people see the outside trappings. I think one of the important things about our culture is respect for others and for our customers. I think it's that mutual respect and I think where the respect is, then the trust can develop so those are some things. Respect is where it starts and all of the others can develop from that. When we are training people, they will ask about handling a mean customer. First of all, a customer is never a problem. A customer is always a customer. We don't know what's going on outside of that customer's day. We want to make sure we always treat our customers with respect, no matter who they are. We want to treat each other with respect. If it's Tony, don't treat Tony any differently than I would treat someone at the coffee shop or who cleans the washroom. That's a hard job and it's just as important and, in some ways, more important than other jobs.

Respect is the key!

CHAPTER FOUR

LEVERAGING TALENTS, GIFTS, AND ABILITIES

"When you become a leader success is all about growing others."

– Jack Welch

The old saying that you are only as strong as your weakest link is never truer when it comes to hiring. Your employees will either make or break your company. In order to build a winning entrepreneurial culture, you must learn how to systematically hire the right fit within your organization.

What is the right fit? The *right fit* is simply defined as the person who has the specific gifts, talents, abilities, and skill set to fulfill the roles and/or responsibilities that have been assigned to them.

Sadly, the challenge that many companies face is hiring when they are going through a massive growth cycle within their business. This is apparently visible when a company is awarded a large contract or when their product is finally accepted into a large retail store *(i.e. Costco, Walmart, or Target)*.

I can remember very vividly having a client who wanted desperately to get their products into one of the big box stores. Their dream was to one day get a call from Walmart asking them to sell their products in their many stores. Be careful what you wish for because you just might get it. In the case of this client, they were in fact invited by Walmart and in order to complete their requirements, they needed to hire bodies fast *(their words, not mine)*.

What I have learned over the last couple of decades, is the ten reasons why many businesses fail. I go into more detail in my book *The Juggling Act: A Step by Step Guide for Balancing Your Business and Your Life*. However, when it comes to growing your business, you have to be careful of 1) Growing too fast and 2) Hiring the wrong people.

It is important, as you grow and expand your company that you consider carefully who you will put into what role. Even when you have to fill orders fast, or you feel like you need to hurry and get more staff in the door to fulfill the contract, do not allow the pressure of fulfilling the orders or contracts to rush you into hiring someone that you will later regret. I cannot tell you how many CEOs have hired people who now basically have them in a hostage situation—one where they are literally afraid to fire the person because of the negative ramifications they believe will arise. We will discuss this in more detail when we talk about building a winning culture through tribe-building in Chapter 8.

I lere is a point to consider. By having a clear hiring process that is designed to build your culture, you will find that not only will you attract rock stars within your organization, these will also become your superstar employees who have a desire to grow and expand with you. It is important that you take the time to hire the right fit for each position and that the people you hire feel like they belong in the role you have placed them in.

A SQUARE PEG IN A ROUND HOLE

During our research, one thing we found was that the companies which excelled had an innate ability to place people in the best roles for their talents, skills, and abilities. Have you ever taken a job that you knew you were over-qualified for, under-qualified for, or just didn't want? I would say that the majority of the people in the workforce would answer, Yes.

I recall one of my first jobs, working at McDonald's Restaurants. At that time I was eighteen, just out of high school, and I really liked money. I loved counting money, as a matter fact, and my first career choice was to be a Certified

Public Accountant. I interviewed with the store manager for the position of cashier, which I was hired for.

They gave me my uniform and I showed up for my first day of work. When I arrived they said, "We had a change of plans. One of our cooks quit, so we need you on the grill." Talk about bait and switch! Well, I needed the job and instead of saying "No thank you, that is not what I was hired to do" *(which is another conversation for a different book)*, I went behind the grill for a grand total of two weeks. I remember dreading every day that I worked at that grill. It's probably one of the reasons why I don't cook now.

The tipping point, or maybe I should say the boiling point, was when I showed up for work early one day, and the restaurant lobby was full of elementary school children flowing all the way out the door. It was a school field trip that had landed at McDonald's for lunch. I will never forget walking through the door into the pandemonium that was going on. There were kids crying, teachers trying to calm them down, people running around behind the registers, bells ringing from the fries that had been placed in the fryer and were waiting to be removed.

My manager saw me walk through the door and started yelling at me at the top of his lungs, "Get back here now!" Have you ever had an experience when everything seemed to be happening in slow motion, almost like the movie *The Matrix*? Well, at that moment I looked at my environment and said to myself, "This is not the job that I applied for. I can't do this." As I was thinking those thoughts, my manager came from behind the counter and said, "I need you to get into your uniform now. What are you waiting for, a special invitation?" That was the breaking point. I looked at him, handed him my uniform, and said "I quit."

This would not be the proudest moment in my life. However, when you have people in the wrong roles, there is no way for them to excel. It is truly like putting a square peg in a round hole. It just doesn't fit.

The challenge for many leaders in hiring is they don't know until after they hire the person that it is a square peg, not a round one. Why? I would say that with the recession and lack of employment, many people are taking jobs that they do not want, just because they feel like they don't have a choice and they need the money.

There are many companies who have had to let go senior level executives, Baby Boomers, and other exceptional talents. We are finding an increase of people who are over-qualified or even deemed by the Employment Department as unemployable. These wonderful people have found your advertisement on CareerBuilder, Monster.com, or Craigslist and they apply knowing that they do not want the position, but feel pressured to find employment. On the flip side, you have college graduates or Generation Y-ers who may view the position as a stepping stone and have no real desire to be in the position long-term.

THE MULTI-GENERATIONAL CHALLENGE

This is the first time in our history when we have three generations working side by side in the workforce. Think about it, as I mentioned earlier we have the Baby Boomers who are deciding not to retire, and who are also living longer and are much healthier than other generations were at their age. The Baby Boomers value hard work and respect. Next, you have Generation X, who watched their parents work their fingers to the bone and sacrifice their lifestyle in order to make ends meet or take care of their families. Gen X values work/life balance. Lastly, we have Generation Y, also known as the Millennials, whom most people think suffer from entitlement. There may be some truth to that, but this group also includes radical, disruptive youth who refuse to play life on anyone's terms but their own. Gen Y values making a greater difference and impact in the world.

As a matter of fact, the 2014 Deloitte Millennial Survey states that "Millennials, who are already emerging as leaders in technology and other industries and will comprise 75 percent of the global workforce by 2025, want to work for organizations that foster innovative thinking, develop their skills, and make a positive contribution to society. The study also reveals that Millennials believe businesses are not currently doing as much as they could to develop their leadership skills and that they need to nurture their future leaders, especially as they cannot count on them biding their time until senior positions arise."[1]

As you can imagine, not only do you have to find the right fit, you also have to know how to effectively coach, communicate, and lead these different multi-generational individuals within your corporate culture.

Where does this leave you, if you desperately need to hire people because of your rapid business growth? How do you make sure you are hiring the right person for the right position? It comes down to one word: assessments.

USING ASSESSMENTS FOR JOB PLACEMENT

Many people have become very skilled at interviewing for jobs. They may be in a situation where they actually *need* rather than *desire* the job they are applying for. Assessments allow you to sort, sift, and separate candidates and truly identify the right fit. The benefit of leveraging assessments in your interview process is being able to capture the interviewee's strengths, talents, and gifts. And more importantly, it determines those things that the candidate least likes to do *(also known as weaknesses)*.

1 https://www2.deloitte.com/content/dam/Deloitte/ global/Documents/About-Deloitte/ gx-dttl-2014-millennial-survey-report.pdf. Accessed 3/18/15.

There are many great tools on the market for taking assessments. Here are some of my favorites:

Myers Briggs Type Indicator *(MBTI)*: Introduced in 1962, this highly recognized assessment has been around for 50 years. Myers Briggs has four main categories *(such as extroversion / introversion and thinking / feeling)*. However, this is one of 16 possible types. The test is used to assess preferences without easy links to strategies or role models, so it really requires an expert to interpret the results and translate them into effective action.

DiSC Profile: Launched in 1928, this system is simpler, and more intuitive. DiSC refers to the four behavior types the test assesses: dominance, influence, steadiness, and compliance. It is more focused on behaviors than preferences, but has the same Jungian roots as MBTI, and there are correlations between the two. Teams find DiSC easier to grasp and explain than MBTI, but both systems lack clear strategies for success, or tailored tools for specific industries or modern challenges.

Strength Finder: Based on a 40-year study of human strengths, Gallup created a language of the 34 most common talents. This assessment is highly recommended by Marcus Buckingham in his book *Now, Discover Your Strengths*. Accompanied by a relevant modern philosophy *(focus on your strengths and you will be happier and more productive for it)*, this test is more prescriptive on proactive strategy than MBTI and DiSC, but lacks an intuitive model that team members can transfer *(few can remember all 34 strengths, let alone how they relate to each other)*. It also does not identify top weaknesses, in either individuals or teams.

Along with leveraging assessments to really identify prospective employees' strengths and skills, it is also important to be able to ask situational questions that dig deeper into the values of the interviewee.

SITUATIONAL INTERVIEW QUESTIONS

Here are some great situational interview questions that will help you identify what matters most to the person you are interviewing:

Interview Question 1: Describe a situation when you had to collaborate with a difficult colleague.

What you are looking for: The "right fit" prospect will demonstrate professionalism in attitude and communication style, along with great problem-solving and conflict-resolution skills.

Red Flag: Someone who blames others, and/or won't accept responsibility or accountability.

Interview Question 2: Describe a situation where you had to work with a difficult manager or important client/customer.

What you are looking for: Candidate's behavior towards authority, communication, emotional stability, and problem-solving.

Red Flag: Someone who comes across as emotionally immature.

Interview Question 3: Describe a situation where you needed to persuade someone to accept your point of view or convince that person to change something.

What you are looking for: Soft skills such as communication, negotiation, leadership, relationship building, and listening ability.

Red flag: Someone who may be abrasive, bullying, or aggressive in communication style.

Interview Question 4: Describe a difficult problem you faced and how you approached it.

What you are looking for: Candidate's ability to collaborate, critical thinking skills, and problem-solving ability. *(Ask about the thought process he or she used to create a solution.)*

Red Flag: Inability to reach out to ask for help.

Interview Question 5: Describe a mistake you've made professionally.

What you are looking for: How candidates learn or reflect on their mistakes.

Red Flag: Inability to admit making mistakes.

Interview Question 6: Describe a situation where you worked under a tight deadline.

What you are looking for: How candidates prioritize and organize workflow, and how they handle themselves under pressure.

Red Flag: Lack of organization, prioritization ability, or time management skills.

Interview Question 7: Describe a time when you received criticism.

What you are looking for: Emotional maturity, leadership potential, adaptability, and ability to learn.

Red Flag: Someone who is a blamer or doesn't take responsibility, or who feels like he or she is being picked on.

Interview Question 8: Describe a situation when you needed to take initiative.

What you are looking for: Someone who is proactive with problem-solving skills.

Red Flag: Someone who doesn't take initiative and does not feel empowered to be proactive. Order-taker *(someone who always waits for instructions because of fear of making mistakes)*.

Interview Question 9: Describe a situation when you've come onto a new team or a new working environment.

What you are looking for: Adaptability and relationship building skills.

Red Flag: Someone who is not adaptable to change or is stuck in his way of doing things.

Interview Question 10: Describe a situation when you needed to work with a client or customer who was very different from you.

What you are looking for: Emotional intelligence and people skills.

Red Flag: Emotional immaturity, prejudice, or judgmental thinking.

By asking these questions, you will get a greater insight and perspective of how the interviewee will think, act, and perform during different situations. I would suggest asking the candidate to give you examples when asking the above questions. Hiring the right fit is step number one; the greater work comes in keeping them. Many employers are concerned that they will invest in the development of an employee, only to make him or her more attractive to their competition. I will discuss this further when we talk about retaining rock star employees. However, just know that if you have a winning culture and you treat and compensate employees well, it is very difficult for the competition to lure them away.

WHAT IS MY CAREER PATH?

As mentioned earlier, one of the reasons why employees quit their jobs is a lack of opportunity for growth and advancement. During my interviews, what came up repeatedly was the employees' opportunity to grow and expand. The "Best Places to Work" companies made an intentional point to give their employees the ability to cross-train in different departments and on many occasions they were challenged by their CEO and other leaders to move into a different position.

When companies are experiencing rapid growth, there are times when an employee may have many job responsibilities that are not listed in the initial job description. What was discovered is that these individuals actually thrive and love that they are being challenged. It is important that you help your employees design a clear career path and show those that you work with that they have an opportunity to advance and grow within the organization.

Do you currently have a career path for your employees? What I recommend is that you create an organizational chart for where you expect your company to be over the next 5 or 10 years. This is easier said than done, only because I know that the marketplace is ever-evolving and with technology vastly advancing for many companies, they are playing catch-up. Don't stress about this exercise—it is a starting point and it will give you an overview of the talent you will need now and in the near future. Also, by doing this you will be able to identify what open positions you will have and determine the potential growth path or opportunities for your employees.

As we know, there is no crystal ball regarding your company's future; however, the clearer you are about the direction you wish to lead the organization in, the more concise you will become in sharing the career path with your employees.

Another suggestion is to ask your employees where they see themselves in the next 3 to 5 years. By doing so, your employees can actually help you create a position based on their strengths, talents, and abilities.

"Great vision without great people is irrelevant." — *Jim Collins*

BRINGING IT ALIVE: ALIGNMENT CHALLENGE 2

Step Two: Leverage Talents, Skills, and Abilities

1. Research and identify top assessment tools to introduce within your company.

   _____

   _____

   _____

2. Take the assessment to discover your own strengths and weaknesses. *(Remember, your strengths give you energy, and weakness is something that drains you... even if you are good at it)*

   _____

   _____

   _____

3. Design an employee's career path based on your current organizational chart.

   _____

   _____

   _____

New Business Culture Revealed: Case Study of "Best Places to Work" — *TRX Training*

TRX: One of the hardest things for a founder, particularly someone like Randy who had no business experience before, was really to apply his values that could be translated across the company, whether that was the first employee or the hundredth. I think here at TRX particularly, the sense of three core values dominates everything that we do, whether it is a conversation with a consumer or internal guidance. They were essentially built around fun, authenticity, and being effective. They have since added a few more.

RMW: I remember your company had an acronym for your values. As I recall, it was F.A.C.E.U.P.

TRX: Right. The core values are around fun, competitiveness, and effectiveness and when we bring someone on they can look at these values and attach themselves to that. One of the important things about any company culture is to allow your employees to live and breathe that.

RMW: Absolutely.

TRX: We get to experience it, whether you are in the TRX class or you can hear people jumping up and down and the music *(referring to on-site TRX training room)*, and it grounds everyone into the culture. Because we need everyone within the organization to be a brand manager.

RMW: It's kind of like you are walking the talk.

TRX: 100%. That's why particularly at a smaller company you need to have people feel like they have ownership of the way the brand is going to develop. And how it's going to be communicated and helping to put guardrails, as it were, around the brand. There are thousands of opportunities every day that are presented and in vetting them, culture plays a large part. TRX has a core 100 employees here, but we have 50,000 personal trainers that have been qualified to train in suspension training, and who are really an extension of our employee base, so it is just as important to give people a sense of culture here as it is across our entire network.

RMW: So what brought you from Nike to TRX?

TRX: Very interesting. I was at Nike, at Levis for a little while, and at Patagonia. Very distinct brands but similar in respect, as you had founders who had a sense of purpose around an ideal and innovation. For me, TRX *(as I considered moving here)* was considerably smaller than I was accustomed to, but having been in the early stages at Nike and watching the explosive reach of the brand, then the business growth that followed, and being in the middle of that curve and being at Patagonia and having seen, arguably, the backside of that curve or the turning of that curve at Levis, I thought TRX was representing a new and fresh perspective on an industry that I think in many ways has stagnated. And through the functional training space and through authenticity of using your body weight to make you stronger, I don't just think it's a physical thing, I think it is also a mental component. It was the product. And the reach that this brand has for being a small company is tremendous. There aren't many companies that have the ability to have the kind of reach and scale that they have, and so those are fascinating to me.

RMW: It's "keep it simple?"

TRX: It is keep it simple, and you begin to expand and grow, you chase things that may make things more complicated at times. I think that a strap is a simple product for the most part. How can you apply that in your business philosophy and everything else? And I do think there is a link between those things. It's something that can be communicated easily.

Let's take a tour....this area is our educational group. These are the people who reach out to our trainers and bring people into our world. So we like to think of our company as not just selling straps in particular. We think of it as selling a triple threat...the hard goods products, the education courses, and the content programming, and each of them helps sell the other. So you use the strap most effectively with the course and content presentation, and if I can show you how to use it you are more likely to use it.

We launched a new program called CORE, which is a membership program to help trainers develop their own businesses including content, education, and programs to help them grow their client bases. A big piece of that is the TRX directory, where you get ranked based on company that drives you to be hired in the directory. And as people search for trainers in the area, it will show the list of trainers and it takes them to their own personal bio and a way for them to increase the client base. These people become our brand ambassadors in many ways.

RMW: Yes. I like to call them your "Marketplace Evangelists." So how do you manage your brand? Specifically, how do you hire the right people, and build your tribe of brand ambassadors *(i.e. rock star employees)?*

TRX: In regards to recruiting, it is similar to the brand ambassadors. It's also a network, a pipeline, it's challenging honestly in a big city like this considering our landscape and being a small private company. It can be challenging because of the core values of the company. It helps us with our attraction, and being listed as a top company to work for provides opportunity to attract great talent, and the fact that we have a great culture and good perks is a tool that we use to bring in good people. We have daily workouts, a lot of people here have different sports that they can develop, and all this adds up to retention and attraction.

I think as we move into how to continue to retain employees, it's a smaller organization where you may not have a broader scope, and the employees do have to do many different things and a greater variety of activities. When I worked at Nike, you had a specific job and that was what you did. Here you have to be open to this "roll up your sleeve" environment which actually helps to grow the employee, whether in developing their own personal resumes or their personal pursuit of physical passion. You have that opportunity to grow.

Culturally, moving from an environment that was more packed, into a more spacious one has been more of a challenge. As you grow, you start to add more room which makes it difficult to scale the culture, and it becomes more important to share the values of the company.

(Introduction of long-term employee)

Kim *(Head of TRX Educational Department)*: I feel like TRX is somewhat unique. When I first started there were only twelve of us and we were all invested in the company doing well. I never heard of any other place where people were so invested and trying to make things grow.

RMW: Let me ask you a question. My assumption is that you worked for other companies to compare with, but you never had this experience before where people were so invested in a company. What was it that made you buy into the company's success? Was it Randy?

Kim: I was being interviewed by a couple of other companies and I saw that TRX had just one product, which is a huge risk at that point. Why would I want to work here? I was like very skeptical, but everyone was. I think most people are looking for a company that has potential and that they can grow with. It's really hard to find that kind of company because a lot of them just crash and burn, and where do you find the one that you can shoot for the stars with? Once I met with Randy, he is very charismatic and he showed me his vision and what he wanted to do in the future and with the culture. I was on-board with that, and also the people at that time were like a really fun group of people that were all eager and I knew I would get to do a lot of different roles since the company was so small at the time. One thing that Randy has always done and I've seen it done as well is there is a ton of opportunity for growth that you may not experience at other places. With me, I probably had 5 or 6 roles in the company, we are constantly moving forward, and some of them were places I wanted to go. If there were certain areas I liked and enjoyed, I had options a couple of times like, "Hey, we are going to have a couple of new positions open, which one would you like?" I went from wearing a million hats to being more focused. So that was kind of nice that I got to create my own path.

RMW: So when you say that you got to create your own path, what I have learned is that where employees got frustrated was when they didn't have an opportunity for growth. So, was there a structured path? Obviously you came at the beginning so it probably was like building the plane as you are flying it. Or was it more like, "Kim, this is the path that we see and we have this whole little career map/blueprint created just for you," or was it that as you grew the opportunity presented itself and you elected which path to choose?

Kim: There were two things that happened and I think it came down to Randy's Navy Seal training. For me, he wants people to move, to expand, to transition their roles, and I deliberately got pushed into roles that I wasn't qualified for. I could have crashed and burned, and at one point they put me in a role just because they didn't have anyone at the time and they said, "Hey, if this doesn't work out you can go back to what you were doing" and they gave that opportunity. But luckily I shined and made it through. Randy doesn't really write people off—if somebody does a horrible job, he either tries to pick people up or find that maybe they are in the wrong position—and they try to shift people around to another place that may be better suited for them. Someone else might say, "You're out of here!"

The biggest thing for me has been the people. I have very strong relationships with the people I work with. We are into teamwork, we all believe in the brand and what it stands for, enjoy seeing how people react, and know that we are doing something that is improving people's lives. You get clients that are 95 years old and people will tell their stories of how someone got hurt in a bombing and lost a leg or were blinded. We had a cool story of one guy who was blind and he trained on the TRX and climbed Mt. Everest. I think there is a lot of inspiration there.

RMW: You have been at this company from the beginning and you have watched it grow and I know that Paul talked about the challenge of maintaining the culture as the company grows. It is bringing in new people and how they blend in with the culture. How do you make sure, if you have a wrong fit, to protect and maintain the brand and the culture when you have new people coming in?

Kim: It has been a challenge. Initially when we were a small company it was easier. We would have an "All Company" meeting, we still do, but in the past we would have them once a week and it was very transparent. Everyone knew everything that was going on. Randy really shared a lot and I think as you get bigger that is risky. He had people who left the company who could potentially share some sensitive information but it definitely makes people feel a lot more a part of it, and new people who come in can say, "Look at all the stuff we are doing." The other thing that we do is F.A.C.E.U.P. to get everyone to embrace the company values. We are pretty good at celebrating our wins and doing teambuilding things.

RMW: What would you say is the best thing about working for TRX Training?

Kim: There are a couple of things. For me it's twofold: I love my actual day to day job. I told this to someone and it's true— I've been here for six years and there has never been a day that I was like, "God I don't want to go to work." It's not just me. Sometimes people will say when something bad happens that "It's just a job." But it's not. Now I have connections with offices around the world. I have connections around the world. It's just like a family. I love the day to day because I get to work on some really cool projects *(the community, the DVD, the CORE program)* which is something the industry has never seen yet. It's kind of like the standard in the fitness industry is pretty low and we are moving into the training industry and it's kind of interesting to see the level that we put out there. Every time we put something out, we are like Apple, it's so new and innovative.

RMW: So the innovation piece is really important to you.

Kim: I think that it is really important. We are changing the game all the time. I feel like, with the project I'm working on, I know that we are the first to do this. So that's really exciting. And also, the people. There is always this sense of comradery and we will go to work out together or we will have a team dinner or happy hour or a competition and we all signed up for this one race to push each other and train for. We also have a training goal that we try to achieve each year. It could be walking to work twice a week or doing the ironman. We are always rooting for everyone.

RMW: So you guys are holding each other accountable too.

Kim: Yes.

RMW: I noticed a lot of collaboration as I was touring your facilities.

Kim: I think it is also flexibility too. Google and some of the other companies have environments where, if you are not in at 8:30am, you are not going to have someone say, "Hey, where are you?" You do your workout but you get your work done. Everyone knows if you come in really late and leave really early, and do your workout at lunch. People are going to know.

RMW: They would say, "Hey what's he doing?"

Kim: Yeah. So there is time when I love having that flexibility where I can take off at 3 pm in the afternoon and come back and stay a little bit later that night and not worry about people saying something. The other thing is my role is more project-based and as long as I get my job done, you have that flexibility.

RMW: It is apparent that the companies that have been interviewing have more of an entrepreneurial culture. And you know an entrepreneur doesn't punch a clock. It's results-based. Let me do my task, take a break, and get back at it. No one is looking for you to punch the clock at 8:00 am, your lunch is at 12:00 pm, and you leave at 5:00 pm. Instead it's, "This is what we are trying to accomplish people, now go out and make it happen," and I give you the flexibility and empower you to create that schedule as long as the team is being supported.

Kim: I do think people are invested and have bought into the company. You have options and you have a vested interest on how the company performs. It makes people more connected and wanting to do well. It is not just that motivation but I think it does help the company because you are part of it and because you have some stock in them.

RMW: Exactly! I worked with a company that I coached and we took them from $250,000 to about $4 million over a 24-month period, and went from 3 to 20 employees. Then they started to offer profit-sharing and it was amazing to see the response of their employees who were vested in the success and acting to bring new business to the organization just because they felt like they were part of the success of the company. Thank you for sharing your insights.

Chapter *Five*

Innovate, Collaborate, or Die

"Change is inevitable; progress is not." – Tony Robbins

THE INDUSTRIAL REVOLUTION IS OVER

As a native Detroiter, I grew up in an environment and a culture that literally thrived and survived from the automotive industry. My father actually retired from Daimler Chrysler after 30 years of devoted service. I remember very vividly growing up, hearing my childhood friends aspiring to work at one of the Big 3 plants when they graduated from college. I remember asking my dad when I graduated from high school to refer me at the plant where he worked. He emphatically declined. As a matter of fact, I recall my dad saying, "No daughter of mine would ever work in a factory."

I never understood why he was so livid and why it was important to both of my factory-working parents to have their

95

daughters working in some plush office. I recall when I was in the 7ᵗʰ grade, my aunt encouraged my mother to make sure that I learned the skill of typing because in her opinion that was my ticket to getting a high paying office job. I share this because, after over 30 years of determining a career path, what my parents intuitively knew *(but didn't know how to describe)* was the end of the Industrial Revolution.

It is clear that we have not been in an industrial revolution for many years. Although we entered the Information Age almost 20 years ago, at times we still maintain the same way of doing business as if we never left the Industrial Revolution.

Think about it. The automotive plant is all about structure, primarily because of mass production. The average person who works inside a factory operates similarly to a robot, which is why robots were able to replace many positions. I am not saying this in a disrespectful manner, more as a matter of fact. Each job position builds upon the other in order to systematically create an end product. The task is repetitive and requires very little or no creativity.

As a society, our children are trained to work in an industrial environment. Our children arrive in school at a certain time; they have bells that move them from class to lunch to class to end of day. It is no different than punching in and out on a time clock, or hearing the bells/whistles that let you know the beginning and end of your shift. The challenge we are facing within our school system is the collaboration, innovation, and creativity that is required for our children to excel in the Information Age.

In order for the U.S. to maintain our leadership in a global economy, the old way of doing things will no longer suffice. It is going to require that we bring a new and fresh way of doing things into our school systems and ultimately into our businesses.

Happily, there are some schools that are on the cutting edge of the educational systems and they are looking at a more collaborative and innovative way of teaching our children. Several schools that are being looked at by our government as models to consider are Cornerstone School in Detroit and High Tech High School in San Diego. These schools innovate the way they are teaching our youth. The programs are designed to challenge the students to partner and collaborate with each other on projects, which is absolutely brilliant. Think about it. In the real world, most people are not sitting at their desks waiting for the bell to ring. They are required to create, brainstorm, and synergize cutting edge ideas to move the company forward. The old paradigm of our education system does not work in this new economy.

DEATH OF THE STATUS QUO AND MEDIOCRITY

To attract a winning entrepreneurial culture, organizations must be willing to bury the status quo and mediocrity mindset. Are you ready to challenge the status quo? Are you willing to step outside of your comfort zone and reach for a new way of doing things? If I look back at the industrial age, the reason why the Big 3 struggled during the recession was because they refused to innovate. They were aware of what their customers were asking them. The customer wanted engine-efficient vehicles and yet Chrysler, GM, and Ford continued to produce gas-guzzling vehicles, while companies like Toyota, Nissan, Hyundai, Lexus, and Tesla dominated the industry, mainly because they gave the customers what they wanted and consistently looked for ways to innovate and create engine efficiency. This is why a company such as Tesla is currently one of the leading automotive companies and new kids on the block. Tesla understands that in order to be the leader in the industry, you can no longer do business the same way as before. Mediocrity equals death in the new business economy.

For many companies, the question I am asked on a regular basis is, "How do you know when it is time to innovate or when to change?"

The answer to this question is based on several factors— one is your industry and the other is your ideal target market. Consider this. If you look at many industries, innovation and the ability to change quickly is essential. For example, the technologies in smartphones are rapidly changing every 4-6 months. There used to be a time when you could have your phone for two years, but now if you keep a phone for one year you will find that it is probably outdated.

Also, it is important to listen to what your customers are asking for. What we know is many businesses spend an exorbitant amount of time chasing new business when the reality is that it takes 70% more effort to generate a new client than retaining and upselling your existing clients.

If you spend time listening to your current or past customers, you will find that they will tell you exactly what they want and you will save time, energy, and effort marketing and creating products or services that they have no interest in.

Another key to helping you innovate and change is also listening to your employees. They are in the trenches and they are listening to what your customers have to say, day in and day out. By collaborating with them you will not only create amazing products and services, but you will keep your employees engaged, motivated, and loyal to your company brand.

A great example of this is when President Barack Obama took office. He realized that there was a lot of money being wasted in the government sector. He also believed that the best ideas usually come from the front line. In 2009, he launched the SAVE Award *(Securing Americans Value and Efficiency)*, in which he sought ideas from federal employees to make the government more effective and efficient and to ensure that taxpayers' dollars were spent wisely.

The winner not only is instrumental in helping save Americans money, but also receives a trip to the oval office to take a picture with the President of the United States. What a great way to get the front line to share their brilliance and get the recognition that they deserve. The first year that the program was introduced, they received over 38,000 entries. The recommendations included something as simple as allowing patients to take medication and supplies that were not being used, home with them instead of throwing them away, or having park rangers deposit monies in a local bank versus shipping it to a bank outside of their area.

What is clear is that if you give people a voice and incentives for them to share their ideas, they will rise to the occasion, especially since the end result is not only good for the company's bottom line, it actually helps to streamline the employees' workflow, making them more effective and efficient.

COLLABORATION IS THE KEY

Many companies are nervous when it comes to this word *collaboration*. It's as if they are afraid they will lose control by doing so. However, the companies that are listed in the "Best Places to Work" not only welcome collaboration, but their cultures thrive because of it.

What does it mean to collaborate? *Collaboration is defined as the action of working with someone to produce or create something.* What I have learned from coaching hundreds of entrepreneurs is the fact that people *buy into* that which they create. If you want to create a dynamic entrepreneurial culture, allow your employees to take ownership in the collaboration, and the creation process will go a long way toward employee retention.

From a practical perspective, some examples of great tech tools to use to support collaboration include Google Drive or Basecamp. These tools allow you to do real time collaboration. If you were to look at what your customers or clients need, how can you collaborate with a like-minded company and create a win-win partnership?

Another great example of collaboration would be with service professionals. If you have an accounting company, who can you partner with that has some of the same clients? Perhaps a business coaching and training company, a financial or wealth planning company, or a law firm. These services would be a perfect synergy for your client and you can actually create a dream team which will not only serve your customers, but you will receive an endless amount of referrals from your other strategic partners. I can also see how a marketing company could partner with a graphic design company or advertising firm. The goal is for you to think outside the box and give some thought as to what products or services your customers really need, so that you can become the trusted advisor and go-to person to meet those needs.

COLLABORATION WITH YOUR CUSTOMERS

Another great way to increase your business is to leverage your community of customers via contests, surveys, social media, and focus groups. Over the last few years, we have noticed an increase of community involvement demonstrated in something like crowd funding. I believe one of the reasons why crowd funding has become very popular is simply because it allows the community to come together for a greater cause or movement. People want to know that their opinions matter and that they are making a difference. This new phenomenon allows people to give voice and support to those things that they believe in, to re-emphasize what was shared in Chapter 1 regarding why people leave. It also gives you a bird's-eye view of why great employees stay. It is through the power of collaboration that an individual, whether an employee or customer, feels like he is helping to grow the brand or company that he believes in.

Consider a company like Frito-Lay, who uses social media to host a contest to choose the next flavored potato chip. The campaign was a brilliant use of leveraging promotion within the grocery stores; they actually gave away free samples of the three finalists' products, made TV commercials where they lead their customers to their Facebook page, and used social media where their fans could actually vote for the flavor they preferred. Frito-Lay fans chose "Chicken and Waffle" and whether we will see this flavor on the grocery shelves is still to be determined. What was impressive is how they leveraged the various marketing channels to engage their customers and, think about it, if you voted and happened to be walking down the grocery aisle only to see your "Chicken and Waffle" flavored chips sitting on the shelf, wouldn't you feel a sense of pride, accomplishment or, if nothing else, nostalgia because your vote and your voice was part of bringing this new product to market? This is the power of collaboration.

LEVERAGE SOCIAL MEDIA TECHNOLOGY FOR COLLABORATION

The example of Frito-Lay is a great illustration of an organization who understands how to leverage technology to deepen relationships and encourage collaboration and engagement with their customers. How can you use the social media technology as a way to collaborate internally with your employees? Remember the age old suggestion box? Is it possible that you can up-level the way your employees provide ideas by using social media platforms to share great ideas?

HOW TO RETAIN ROCK STAR EMPLOYEES

Do you want to know one of the secrets to retaining ROCK STAR employees? Give them a voice, a cause, a purpose, an opportunity to grow, and watch what happens. At the end of the day, when a Level 4 Culture employee leaves his job to go home at night, he wants to know without a doubt that his contribution matters. This employee's motivation is not solely to get a paycheck, it is to make a difference. He has a desire not only to be good, but to be exceptional.

IS "GOOD TO GREAT" GOOD ENOUGH?

One of the most famous business books of all time is *Built to Last* by Jim Collins. This book examines the top companies of our time to find out what they specifically did to outlast the competition. What's interesting is, if you look at the companies that were being examined, you will notice that many of these companies are no longer in existence or they are struggling to keep their doors open. How is that possible? What did they do wrong? It comes down to being too comfortable and being afraid of innovation.

The challenge with being on top is that sometimes we can forget there is someone beneath us who is climbing the mountain and looking to overthrow us. In our current economy, being good is not good enough. What the consumer is looking for and what your future employees are looking for is to work for a company that is exceptional. They are looking for a company that endeavors to be GREAT.

The beautiful thing about technology is that it has leveled the playing field and even an army of one can create a product and deliver service in such a great way that they will create a loyal fan base and followers. I can hear you saying, "Rae, I don't have the income, people, or resources to deliver GREAT." Here's the sad truth—there are so many business that are delivering subpar, mediocre products and services that when you show up and commit to delivering a good product in the consumers' eyes, it looks like a "great" product.

Think about this example. Tony Hsieh built a billion dollar company simply by wanting to deliver excellent customer service in a world where customer service is not only bad in many cases, it is non-existent. Tony was able to set himself apart from the competition and create what some would call a "blue ocean" strategy. What is the blue ocean strategy? It is when you decide that you are not going to compete with others in an overcrowded, oversaturated, noisy industry, and you will do something so unique and different that you create your own category. Another perfect example of a company that uses the blue ocean strategy is Cirque du Soleil. If you want to know more about how to differentiate yourself and create something radically and simply unique, I would encourage you to pick up the book *Blue Ocean Strategy* written by W. Chan Kim and Renee Mauborgne.

As you can see, when you think about innovation and collaboration, it doesn't have to be daunting. To innovate is simply to take that which you have already created and find different, new, or improved ways of doing it. We are currently in a connected economy and people are already collaborating online and outside of their workplace. Your goal as a leader is to provide the openness needed to make collaboration an essential part of your organization. And to provide feedback on the results, so employees can see the impact of their collaborative effort. Openness only happens with TRUST, clearly defined goals, and a shared sense of value. In the following chapters, you will learn how to create a company environment that fosters openness, creativity, and an entrepreneurial spirit.

"Coming together is a beginning, staying together is progress, and working together is success."

– *Henry Ford*

BRINGING IT ALIVE: ALIGNMENT CHALLENGE 3

Step Three: Innovate, Collaborate, or Die

1. Where do you find yourself being stagnated within your organization?

   _____
   _____
   _____

2. Can you introduce an employee program similar to the SAVE program that rewards creative ideas that either increase efficiency, save money, or add to the bottom line? If so, brainstorm some ideas of what incentives you would give your employees.

   _____
   _____
   _____

3. Create a collaboration program that involves your customers, clients, or strategic partners.

   _____
   _____
   _____

4. How can you leverage ROCK STAR employees so they feel like they are adding value to the company?

   _____
   _____
   _____

Chapter Six

IF YOU AND YOUR COMPANY ARE NOT GROWING...

"Begin with the end in mind." — *Steven Covey*

WHAT'S THE FINISH LINE?

I've had the great fortune of working with some amazing entrepreneurs and small business owners. One thing I have noticed is a trend in which people built wildly successful companies and yet they had no joy from the experience and, in fact, hated what they were doing. How is that possible? It is because they are out of alignment with what matters most to them, and it is also because they do not have a clear vision of what the end looks like.

My story is no different than many small business owners. I became an entrepreneur because I really wanted the freedom to choose and create the lifestyle that I desired. However, what happened was far from what I really wanted. If I am to be transparent, I found myself hitting what I like to call the proverbial wall. I was doing all of the right things and making really great traction, but I was unfulfilled. Was this all there was to success? There had to be more, right? The truth is, I didn't have a clear vision of what the finish line looked like—also known as an "exit strategy."

So, what is your exit strategy? Are you building your business to sell or are you planning to give it to your children? Are you planning to go public? What does the end look like in your business? Do you plan on making a billion dollars or would you be happy with ten million dollars?

It is vitally important that you know where you are trying to go and have a map of your destination. Can you imagine going on a trip across the country with no map or GPS? Probably not, and yet that is exactly what many leaders do in their businesses. This is your opportunity to really create a business that you love, to go back to the drawing board and ask yourself the questions above, in order to make sure that what you are creating is going to meet your needs both personally and professionally.

ESTABLISHING MEASURABLE GOALS

Once you know where you are going in terms of your exit strategy, the next step is to create and document clear, measurable goals. The key word in this phrase is "measurable." You may have heard the phrase, "you can't improve what you can't measure." Unless your goal is documented *(written)* and consistently reviewed *(measured)*, you will discover it very difficult to reach your company's goals on a regular basis. It is similar to a company who creates a mission and vision statement or a business plan and then lets it sit on the bookshelf without ever being visited again.

The organizations that I had the pleasure to interview were relentless about goal-setting. What was even more impressive was that the goals were actually displayed on the wall where everyone could see them, and they were re-evaluated either on a daily, weekly, or bare minimum monthly basis and compared to the actual results that the company achieved.

Posting your goals in clear view of your employees reminds them of what they should be focused on. It is not just the CEO, C-Level executives, or managers' responsibilities to reach the goals of the company. It is everyone's responsibility to actively pursue the company's goals, outcomes, or objectives. It goes back to the Level 4 Culture where the employees feel like they are *all in it together.* There is a sense of buy-in and thus there is a feeling of doing one's own part to help the company reach its target.

WHAT GOALS SHOULD YOU ESTABLISH FOR A WINNING ENTREPRENEURIAL CULTURE?

When you think about establishing measurable goals to grow an amazing business, the first thing that many people do is focus on the revenue goal. I would suggest that you do the same—however, I would also recommend that you add why this goal is important to achieve. For example, Infusionsoft has a revenue goal to reach a billion dollars in revenue. However, this income goal is in *alignment* with their mission, which is to help small business owners to be successful. When they achieve their goal it will be simply a scorecard of the work that they have accomplished in the small business owner space.

By establishing the "why" of achieving a particular goal, you are actually creating a built-in motivator to pursue the goal. When I am coaching CEOs, executives, and small business owners in creating S.M.A.R.T. goals, the first thing we do is to make sure the goal is specific, measurable, achievable/attainable, realistic *(to them)*, and time-based. This is a term that you have probably heard before. However, I would also ask you how many times you have created a goal and not achieved it. Let's go even deeper—how many times have you created a S.M.A.R.T. goal and not achieved it?

There are three things I have observed that prevent many people from reaching their goals. The first reason is that many people do not set a goal that is realistic for them. A perfect example of this is with one of my one-on-one coaching clients who had a desire to take his business from zero to $1 million dollars in revenue in twelve months. Not only did he accomplish the goal, but we were able to do it in ten months. When I share this case study at one of my live trainings, I am always approached by attendees afterwards who want to know the exact strategy I used to help him to achieve these amazing results. I definitely had a strategic blueprint that I coached him through to get there, but the #1 reason he was able to accomplish this goal in the timeline we set was because the client was in total alignment and 100% congruent around the belief that he *could* reach the million dollar mark in a 12-month period *(even if he was starting from scratch)*. The first question you need to answer when you are crafting your goals is this, "Is this goal realistic to you?"

The second reason that prevents people from achieving their goals is lack of accountability. You see, you can have a goal that is measurable like in the above example–the goal was to reach $1 million dollars in twelve months. It was truly a S.M.A.R.T. goal based on the definition. The problem around goal-setting that I see with many people is they are great at setting the goal; however, there is no one to hold them accountable. There is no one who is asking them how they are doing on a regular basis to make sure that they are on the right track. The beautiful thing about accountability is that if you have it on a regular basis and you find that you are off track, you have the opportunity to make a mid-course correction or the necessary adjustments in order to reach the target.

What I have just shared are two of the reasons that keep people from reaching goals. These two can mean the end to anyone's dreams to achieve amazing results. However, the third reason is the one that makes all the difference in the world, and that is…

SETTING GOALS WITHOUT PURPOSE

You might think by now that I sound like a broken record. The truth of the matter is, more employees are quitting their jobs, and even CEOs are jumping ship and turning over their reins, in search of careers with more meaning. What's the point of making a living, if you don't have a life? Why make a lot of money if there is no meaning to be gained from the company? There is a new trend that is surfacing from the recession. This new breed of business that is rising from the ashes of company layoffs, downsizing, and bankruptcies, includes companies with a cause. These are companies that are committed to not only creating wealth and employment; they are doing it while also doing good in the world. These companies have a meaning and a purpose, and their primary motivation is not just to make money, it is to do so by adding massive value to their clients, stakeholders, and the planet.

This may sound foo-foo or altruistic. You may be asking, "Is it really possible to do this and be profitable?" The answer is an unequivocal "Yes!" There were many benefits to come out of a down economy, and one of them is how consumers look at the dollar that they are spending. In today's economy, consumers are demanding that those companies they choose to spend their dollars with have values that are in alignment with what they believe. And social media has made it very easy to find out who is authentic and who is playing the cause-based marketing game.

Consider this. If you had a choice, would you choose to buy your pair of shoes from a store that didn't have a cause or would you want to spend your money with a company that, for every pair of shoes purchased, donated another pair to a child in a third world country? If you ask the majority of consumers, all things being equal, they would prefer to spend their money to do business with someone like Blake Mycoskie, CEO of TOMS Shoes. Blake started the company after spending time in a remote, indigenous village near the Brazilian border where he noticed that most of the children there had no shoes. Not only were they cutting and bruising their feet when they walked long distances to fetch water for their households, many were missing school because they're not allowed to attend barefoot. In some families, they owned only one pair of shoes and everyone had to share them.

This story may seem far-fetched, especially when you think about how blessed you are to live in a country like the United States. I recalled my mother sharing similar stories about her growing up in Kansas City, Missouri and being unable to leave the house because they only had one pair of shoes. She would have to take turns with her sister to leave the house. Based on this story, do you think my mother would have hesitated to buy her shoes from TOMS, knowing that she was doing good by supporting a company that also does good in the world?

In the new corporate economy, there is an expectation that the companies that consumers support and employees choose to work for, will be companies with a heart to make a greater impact and a greater difference in their communities. This impact can be at a local, national, or global level. It is no longer business as usual.

What other measurable goals should you consider creating for your organization? I would suggest creating goals that are based on your company's mission, vision, and values. The company's mission and vision are directly related to why you do what you do. We will discuss this further in Chapter 10, when we talk about aligning your values for impact. However, the company's values are all about *how* you do what you do. How do you show up as a leader? How do you show up as a company? How do you interact and treat your employees? How do you treat your clients and customers?

As you establish your company's goals, it is also important that you bring your employees' opinions into the discussion. What will their part be in achieving the overall outcomes and objectives of the company? What are their specific roles, responsibilities, and duties? The more clarity you provide for your team, the more opportunities you will give your superstars to rise to the challenge of achieving optimal RESULTS.

ACCOUNTABILITY IS WHAT THEY CRAVE

I mentioned earlier how accountability plays a major role when it comes to the reason why many goals are not achieved. I also had the opportunity to interview many employees from top companies, as well as some corporate escape artists, to find out what made them stay while others were running straight for door. Many of the reasons why employees quit were covered in Chapter 1. However, one of the reasons that surprised me the most had to do with the areas of growth and the lack of accountability.

Many companies have goals to hire the best talent in their industry. What you must learn about superstars is their need to be challenged. Many superstars are competitive in nature. They are competing primarily against themselves, and thus they need and want to be challenged. They also want to be part of something bigger than themselves. It is important to them to know the goals that the company is trying to reach, their part in reaching the goals, *and* they want to be held accountable for these goals. Nothing frustrates a superstar employee more than receiving an assignment, task, or project—or even worse, attending a "dead-end" meeting with no deadlines, no target dates, or no objectives. Hear me when I say that your superstar and rock star employees want to be held accountable. As a matter of fact, they crave accountability. Why? It gives them an opportunity to showcase their talents and decision making skills, ask for assistance if needed, and give valuable feedback for achieving the task at hand.

I think this would be great time to define accountability. Accountability is defined as *"actions towards or involving others that reflect the integrity of the person you want to be."* But please note, there is a huge distinction between accountability and micromanagement. If you want to know a management style that is most destructive to your culture, it is that of micromanaging. Webster's dictionary defines a micromanager as a person who manages "especially with excessive control or attention to details." A better definition is from the Urban dictionary which defines a micromanager as a person who is "driven by fear and anxiety into meddling with others' work." I think that this is a better description and explains the root cause of micromanagement, which is fear, or lack of trust.

Is there ever a time when you need to become a micromanager? I will say there are a few exceptions. One would be when you are first training someone on a new competency and you may want to take more time with the individual to make sure that you are setting her up for success. The other exception would be when you have an employee who may be on a performance plan for poor performance. You may, for a short time, choose to micromanage this employee. The key phrase is "for a short time." If you find yourself constantly micromanaging your employees, it may be a great time to look in the mirror and ask yourself the question as the leader, "What is really going on with you?"

Micromanaging is not only detrimental to your company culture, it will absolutely not be tolerated by superstar employees. They will either call you on it or they will simply leave.

HOW TO CHALLENGE SUPERSTARS, ROCK STARS, AND OTHER A-PLAYERS

Now that we know how to create measurable goals and the importance of accountability in working with superstar employees, it is also important to learn exactly how to challenge them.

The best way to challenge a superstar, rock star, or A-player is to get them involved in building the company. A perfect example of this is when I worked for a coaching company that created a Coaching Advisory Board. This board was established to give the leadership information about what was actually happening on the coaching floor, with our coaching clients, and with the programs that were being ramped out. We were responsible to be the voice of the coaches who elected us. That's right! Each person who was part of the Coaching Advisory Board was voted for by our peers, not management. We had monthly meetings and we shared with the leadership team the struggles that we saw on the horizon. We also got to share the successes, as well as anything we felt that would be innovative and would help the company to grow.

Being part of the advisory board also gave the company an opportunity to roll out beta programs, products, and services and get our feedback. It truly was a win-win and it also keep all of us superstars, rock stars, and A-players involved, engaged, and loyal to the company's objectives. Why? It is simply that people support that which they create. The company was ingenious by creating this within the culture, because they brought the influencers *(that the employees respected)* and placed them in a leadership role that allowed for innovation, growth, and open communication within the organization.

Another example to challenge your superstar employees is to create a committee that you can put them in charge of. What goals or initiatives can you ask them to step up and play a leadership role in? Many companies are worried that by doing so they are going to get demands for more money. That's usually the furthest thing from the truth. Remember, when it comes to employees quitting, lack of compensation was on the list but it was far beneath the opportunity to grow, be challenged, and be appreciated. Google gives their employees time during their work hours to create new innovations which have nothing to do with their current positions. They get to work on any project they want. Not only does this create engagement and foster innovation, it also keeps those high achievers from being bored and starting their own startup on the side. It really comes down to allowing them the opportunity to grow and expand.

What about offering a continuing education stipend as part of an employee benefits package? There are companies listed on the "Best Places to Work" that give a certain amount per year for the employee growth plan. These monies can be used either on educational courses that are directly related to their career track, or training that fosters work/life balance *(i.e. coaching certification, cooking classes, etc.)*. Is it worth offering an additional $1,000 per year or a tuition reimbursement package to keep your top employees?

What we know is that when you lose a top employee, the replacement cost is sometimes twice that employee's current salary, not to mention the fact that this person could actually become your competition. It is not about your being held hostage to your employee; rather it is about your understanding that typically superstar employees are entrepreneurial in spirit. If you can give them an opportunity to leverage their entrepreneurial spirits within your organization, you will find that they remain loyal and wouldn't dare think about leaving you for the competition or their own business.

I recall a training that I did with T-Mobile managers when I asked them to define a great manager. One of the managers shared a story of how one of his leaders *(mentors)*, early on in his career with T-Mobile, invested in him by sending him to a high level training course. He stated "because the company was willing to invest in me, I would forever be indebted and would never leave." What was communicated here not only works in business, it also works in life. It is a simple and really uncomplicated truth that when you do right by your employees, they will in return become loyal, raving fans and do the right thing for the company and for the clients.

"Without continual growth and progress, such words as improvement, achievement, and success have no meaning."
– *Benjamin Franklin*

BRINGING IT ALIVE: ALIGNMENT CHALLENGE 4

Step Four: Growing through Goal-setting is Critical

1. How does your organization challenge your rock stars and emerging leaders to grow? What are some ways that you can support your employees' career paths?

   _____

   _____

   _____

2. Do your employees know what your company's goals are? Are your goals in alignment with your company's mission and core values?

   _____

   _____

   _____

3. What internal/external programs can you introduce within your organization to increase growth through goal-setting? *(i.e. leadership development training, coaching, team building, etc.)*

   _____

   _____

   _____

New Business Culture Revealed: Case Studies from the "Best Companies to Work For" —*Infusionsoft*

RMW: So as I mentioned, I am interviewing companies, and primarily what we are doing is, we are looking at companies that have winning cultures to find out what they do differently. What we know is, the U.S. Department of Labor stated that two million employees quit their jobs each and every month and it's not because they want to start a business, it's because they are not happy where they are. So if you were to define a winning culture, how would you define it?

Clate Mask *(CEO/Co-founder of Infusionsoft)*: I would say it's a defined culture, so I think the challenge with creating winning cultures is that the leaders don't take the time to truly define what it means to fit inside the company culture; this isn't theory, this is having gone through an experience. Earlier on, when we had only a handful of employees—four or five employees—I'd say "Okay, now next year we are going to grow to ten employees," and people would say, "How are we going to keep this great family culture we have?" And I would say, "It will be okay, don't worry." And next year I would say, "Okay, we are going to go to eighteen employees this year," and people would say, "I'm just worried that we are not going to keep this great culture," and I would say, "It's okay, don't worry."

And year after year we grow that way, and people would come to me and literally, it got to the point where almost a week wouldn't go by when somebody would ask me, "How are we going to keep this great culture as we get there, because you always talked about these visions and plans of what we are doing?" and I would say, "Don't worry, we'll figure it out, it will be fine."

And then when we decided that we were really going to build the company and go forward and become the standard of sales marketing software for small business, that meant we were going to raise venture capital. And when we decided that we were going to raise venture capital, that meant we were going to bring in a lot of employees, and then I started going, "Okay, how are we going to keep this great culture?" *(Laughing)*

RMW: So, at that point, how many employees did you have when you made the decision that you were going to bring in venture capital?

CM: We had about fifty employees.

RMW: Okay. And at that time, did you have your mission, your purpose, your vision?

CM: No, so that's my point. The company was small enough and we were tightening enough at fifty employees that we were doing just fine bringing in good people, and the vibe was there. We had the culture, but we just hadn't defined it, to really call it out. And then what happened, when we decided that we were really going to go forward and raise venture capital that meant we were going to hire a lot of people. I started just going on the hunt for how to do this and I read a bunch of different things and a lot of roads took me to Jim Collins's work.

RMW: Yeah, that's great.

CM: Yes it's great. And in just the work you had done, I started to find, to kind of discover that discipline of organizational design and organizational development, and it's so funny, because when I was in business school we had to take organizational behavior classes and nobody liked these classes. It would be like "ahhh!" But it was looked down upon and I had been out of school long enough, I had been running a business long enough to realize that actually this is the stuff that makes it all work, and I started to find organizational design and organizational development as a real discipline of professionals.

Then I found a guy who was trained in that and he actually attended a TIE event that I was speaking at. I think TIE stands for The Indus Entrepreneurs. It's a group of Indian-born nationals from India that started it and it's way broader than India, but it's kind of a technology in India coming together in America and creating a group around that and they are all over now, TIE is all over. But it's really big in the South Korean tech center. We have a TIE group in our zone and they asked me to speak, because we just raised venture capital and it was just this big deal because we were bringing in venture capital in their zone from South Korea and that didn't happen very often. So I was speaking and this organizational development guy was there and I started talking to him, we had lunch, and I realized okay, I need someone like this. At the time, I was kind of the manager of the culture and I had a great co-founder in Scott, who was helping me to do that, just be a kind of a spiritual leader of a buddy but there was no other intentionality to it. So we got to that point and I met Brad and Bradamar's Consultants, and within a few months Bradamar was a full-time employee—we call him our "build to last" director.

RMW: Oh, nice.

CM: And his job was to just help us do all of the things in the company that keep that culture strong, that keep the wedges that naturally happen between employees and managers to not happen, you know—it's little stuff, it's dumb stuff, it's things like management parking spaces and dumb little status things and perk things that managers or executives are going to have and that they shouldn't have.

RMW: You know, it's funny, I had the chance to interview Zappos for the book and you know, walking through their facilities you go through there, and Tony is right there, center-stage. You know, they don't have offices that look down on the staff, which is one of the things that they shared with me in regards to their building. So you define the culture now and you have this amazing culture, you have all of these people, but now you've got money so you've got to bring in people really fast, right, so how do you protect the culture?

CM: Great, great, and by the way Zappos was one of the companies we really studied, we did the tour and then they created their program called Zappos Insight. We were in the very first group of that and a bunch of our staff and I talked to Tony. I went to lunch with him and I asked him, how do you build a culture when you get venture capital and we had a conversation about that. What we have learned is, and I say this in a very concise phrase that it's probably not fair that I say this so concisely. It is this: we hire and train and fire to the purpose, values, and mission. So we define the purpose, values, and mission and then we literally screen for that in the hiring process and we have people checking it, and we do all sorts of stuff to get them to make sure that they really do have passion to help small businesses succeed, and that they really go about their work embracing the values that we set, and to say all the time, these are our 9 core values and you have got 97 values and I have 86 values and Ray got 112 values and that's fine, but we better share these 9, and if you don't share these 9, it doesn't mean you are a lesser person, it just means that you don't fit here. There are places where they have some values stated or unstated but they are going to resonate with you better and you are going to fit better there, and so we try to help people see that.

In the hiring, training, and firing process there is such a stigma associated with being let go and there is so much fear and worry around it, the reality is that you just find a place where you absolutely love it and you know the discussion of corporate responsibility goes on. The major corporate area of responsibility that companies don't make clear is who it is that belongs here.

RMW: Exactly.

CM: If they actually make that clear, it is such a service to people, it is such a service to their employees, it's such a service to their customers, and leaders don't do that sometimes. We decided earlier on that we are not going to do that, we are going to make it clear, we are going to define it and we are going to hire to it and when they come in they come in because we believe in addition to possessing the skill set or the role that we hire them to do, they have this cultural fit, and we do a two-day or two-week intensive training and at the end of that two weeks, we make them an offer. We say, you can have $5,000 to leave today, or you can choose to stay onboard; we give it to them on a Friday, at the end of two weeks and then they have to think about it over the weekend, talk with their families or their friends, and then come back and they have to give us a written acceptance or denial of our offer. We have only had two people who accepted, ever.

RMW: Oh wow.

CM: We love that they accepted because it's awesome. But the best part is that people who deny that offer, they are making a real decision, and for many of these people they are coming into a job that's going to pay them $30,000 a year and so we are saying $5,000 right now, so it's a big deal. That's on the hiring side, but then on the training side, we know that nobody is a perfect fit in all my values. I'm not a perfect, perfect fit on my values. I have my days where I might be perfect and other days where I am not perfect and I need to be better in those areas, so we work on them, and we have a leadership development team that works on them. It's a one-man shop in the "build to last" preservation department, if you want to think of it that way. Now there are about twelve to thirteen people there in leadership development. We have created a leadership model that is kind of the higher standard of our purpose, values, and mission for the leaders, because leaders are the ones who actually train people, get people to not just manage performance, but leading to the purpose, values, and mission and making sure that people fit. And when there is something that's off, correcting that quickly, working and coaching them through it. There's a lot of coaching that goes on, and if we can't coach and train someone through an area where they just got a little bit off on the purpose, values, and mission, then we get them out of there and we do it quickly. It's not because we don't care about them, it is because we care way more about the people who are here.

RMW: Exactly. It's almost like if you let them linger, they will become poisonous, it's almost like that old saying about the bad apple, and it really does spoil the bunch.

CM: Yes, yes absolutely, and so it's not that they are bad people, it's just that they are not the right fit, and so we hire, train, and fire to support our mission. And you asked, How do you find a way to cultivate it? You define it. How do you preserve it? You hire, train, and fire to support the mission. I could talk to you for hours, you could come visit our company, you could see what we do and realize that we are intense about this stuff.

RMW: Do you find that because you are so defined and because of your sense of accountability, that even if managers or leaders are not watching over them, the employees will rise up and challenge others by asking, "Are you living accordingly?"

CM: Absolutely, absolutely, and I mean entirely. So that's a part of what happens, is that you just start to build a self-reinforcing—I don't like the term self-policing—it's self-reinforcing, and we went through a stage where it was a little bit of finger-pointing, "Well you are not doing this" and I said, "Hold on, our values are that we empower entrepreneurs. These are our values and they all start with 'we,' but they are really meant to be 'I.' They aren't meant to be 'you' statements, but 'I' statements, so get the beam out of your own eye." So we went through some of that, a little bit like judgment and self-righteousness around values and some of that stuff, but we worked through that, and we found out that there is a little issue when people are doing that. It takes a little bit out of our values in doing that, because it's really intended to be an introspective thing.

RMW: It's funny you say that. I used to work for a company where one of the core values was "Excellence is our minimum standard. If it's not excellent don't do it." We had a project where we were planning to mail something to our entire database and one of the periods in the direct mail piece was missing. Someone forgot the period and 6,000 pieces were going to get mailed, and I remember someone stating that they were not going to mail theirs because there was no period. Why? Because this is not excellent and we are not living our core values.

What defines excellent? Excellent is doing the best that you can with the information that you have within the time frame allowed. We are okay; it's just a little period.

CM: So that would become a part of self-reinforcing and it also becomes very self-forcing from the inside. And on the outside it's very magnetic in its nature, meaning it's attracting the right people and repelling the wrong people.

RMW: Absolutely.

CM: And the power of a magnet is not just as an attraction, it's a repellent too.

RMW: Absolutely. It's like identifying that ideal client because your core values are identified and because people know that they are going to come into the culture and environment, and your environment is always going to trump your willpower. Either they will stay or they will leave.

CM: Yes, yes.
RMW: So we know that a lot of employees leave because of lack of growth. What do you guys have in place to challenge and encourage your employees' growth?

CM: Wow, so one of our values is that we innovate constant and never-ending improvement and I've said for a long time, if you are not interested in growing, then this is not a place for you. So part of what we do is to make it very, very clear on the front end, we hire growers and we make it very clear to our people inside if you are not growing, we are sorry but we don't want you occupying a seat because there is somebody else who is a grower and who wants that seat. He is going to make that seat better and when you are a company that is growing as fast as we are, you can only grow as fast as your people and your capabilities are growing. I am not a believer in "we hire all of those capabilities," that's bull. You grow the capabilities and you add capabilities as you need them, but if you are not growing the capabilities first, then that is not the way most companies grow.

I had to reprogram my board members' brains to see that, and it took years to do, but I had to reprogram their brains to see that you grow a company over the long term by growing the people, by growing the leaders. Their mentality was, oh this person is just not growing, this person is here for three years so we are not growing them. No, and I am not saying that doesn't happen sometimes, but their default is to hire a person, get the use out of them and when you have outgrown what they are used to, let's hire this executive because he has been to the stage of $2M to $50M in revenue, and once we get to $51M in revenue, we should let that person go. That's just the mentality and I'm like, well, I've never been through what I'm going through, and I have no idea the stuff I have to be doing in five years, but I will know by the time I get there. You can count on that.

RMW: Wow, I will prove it.

CM: And I will always say it like that. The first time I said it to my

134

board members they were like, wow. I said this to my team all the time, I am not a good enough CEO for running Engineering but you can bet your last dollar I will be good enough by the time we get there. I am just driven to get better and better, and that's just one of the things about me. I don't know, for whatever reason, I love it. I just love personal development and growth and I can't imagine not working to get better and better every day.

So I set that tone for the executive team and I say all the time it's a fast-moving train, and I will be doing you a huge disservice if I give you any impression other than you've got to get better and better and better or the train will just run you over. Because one thing I am totally committed to is, if you are just not going `to achieve the vision that we have, I need to get somebody else in place who is going to grow fast enough. I'm harsh in the sense that I am saying there is no comfort in growth, so if you are looking for a comfort zone and you are looking for a nice stable status quo, then you shouldn't be in a technology company that is growing 50% per year, because you are going to get run over. If you are the grower and you believe in this and you establish our values that we innovate in constant and never-ending improvement, then I constantly improve and it attracts others to come into an environment like that.

RMW: Absolutely.

CM: If you are not a grower, it's threatening to come into an environment like that. You are always wondering if the company is going to pass you up. How long am I going to be able to prove that I am good enough to be here? Well, growers don't feel that way, they are just like "Hey, I'm ..."

RMW: Go, make it happen.

CM: Yes, so that's the answer for us because we are a growing company and that means our people are growers.

RMW: Do you have a specific career path or track?

CM: Yes, great question, some do. Some want to go to the leaders and we had to really help people to see that growing doesn't mean that you have got to become a manager or director, that's not what growing means. Growing means taking on bigger and greater responsibilities, whatever that is. It might mean that you develop and your role still may be the same but what you actually do is taking on new technology. There are just all kinds of ways to grow. What you really need to be doing is increasing your ability to serve our customers...

RMW: ...and looking at your skill set.

CM: Yes, yes. So there are some people that are going more down a leadership track, there are some people that have more of a deep expertise in their area, and there are some people that want to go all across the board. We have people who are just bright-eyed and eager and want to learn stuff in many different areas, and we love those people because they will get into something and figure it out, so we have different ways that people grow.

RMW: I know you have to run. How do you keep your employees? One of the things that we learned from companies that have winning cultures is, when they have the people who have been with them from the beginning, they didn't have all the perks, but the people who now join the fruit of their labor sometimes have a sense of entitlement. How do you keep your company from falling into an entitlement trap?

CM: Oh, boy, such a great question. I wish we could talk about this for a long time, because I don't have all the answers and we work on this a lot. One of the things is, we really teach people and we say our number one value is we empower entrepreneurs. We are talking about the entrepreneurial spirit, we are not talking about just people that own a business. We are talking about our employees that are creators, who are improving things. The reason why we revere entrepreneurs is because entrepreneurs get paid for results, not efforts.

RMW: Absolutely.

CM: And so when we teach that, we say the opposite of entrepreneurship is entitlement and we just help people understand, if you find yourself slipping into entitlement, which by the way everybody does, they are human characteristics. This is one of the shameful things that we do, and we need to check that and we need to think about that. The reason why I said that I don't have all the answers is because we are always working on it. We'll have a time when things are really going great for a year and then this nervousness starts to creep in, it happens in certain individuals, and the trick is that's what you've got to train to. You have to train to the value of entrepreneurship, you've got to train to the value of anti-entitlement, which is empowering entrepreneurs. There is no entitlement in entrepreneurs, not in the successful ones, so we try to teach that. It's really interesting though because what we have seen over the years is that it goes in waves and we have times of entitlement and it's a very interesting thing. It is kind of perceived as a difficult time, so only if you are really good does it go like that. We can nip that in the bud quicker and we are going to prevent ourselves from going into a drought.

I mean, companies don't grow like this, and one of the things that pronounces that gift is the characteristic of entitlement. And we are trying to do that because I would be happy with this, you know. I notice that they tend to be long cycles, they are like 6 to 18 month things, you know, they are not like weekly or monthly, but are longer and so we work on trying to get better and better at it. The one thing I do know is that it is kind of a precursor to a fall and when you see it in the culture and you are feeling more entitlement, I get very nervous because I know what that turns into.

RMW: The last question.

CM: Yes.

RMW: So, you have been in business for how long?

CM: The company's been in business for 12 years.

RMW: For 12 years, so if looking at that person about to start, what advice would you give yourself?

CM: I am so sorry, I don't mean it this way, but I would say, "Go read Conquering Chaos, the book I wrote about because it's....

RMW: Great book, by the way.

CM: Oh, thank you.

RMW: Very relevant.

CM: Thank you, I am glad you liked it. But just those years of struggles, those mindset struggles you deal with, because when you are first starting it's the mindset stuff that beats you up—it's the doubts and fears and concerns and the darkness and all of the financial pressure, that just beats the creativity out of you and you have to keep yourself on top of that game mentally. It is a game, a total game, and it's what you say to yourself and what you allow others to say and what you allow to get inside of that sacred space, that has everything to do with your potential for success, and yet an entrepreneur begins to see that and has plenty of time to be thinking.

RMW: Absolutely. I tell my clients that 80% of your success has nothing to do with talent, skill, or abilities, but the conversations you have.

CM: Absolutely.

RMW: So thank you, I am going to let you go.

CM: Thank you for talking to me, I surely appreciate it.

Chapter Seven

BUILD IT AND THEY WILL COME

---

*"You don't need to convince everyone. All you need to do
is motivate people who choose to follow you."*

– Seth Godin

THE POWER OF TRIBE-BUILDING

One of my favorite movies is *Field of Dreams* with Kevin Costner. Remember the scene where he was told "if you build it, they will come?" This is how many small business owners and entrepreneurs begin with a dream, and what happens to many is their dream rapidly becomes a nightmare simply because they do not have a sound strategy for business growth. There are many companies that have a ton of customers and clients, and yet they struggle to meet deadlines and deliverables, or the client they are supporting is not their ideal client."

Tribe-building is one of my secret weapons in helping those that I coach and consult with to really create the business of their dreams. Seth Godin wrote a great book entitled *Tribes*, where he defined the three major components of finding and building a tribe. They consist of:

1) A Leader
2) A Group
3) An idea, thought, or concept

When you are looking at tribe-building, however, the key component that you must be aware of is the fact that tribes *(or groups)* are already being created within your organization. The Internet and social media were really designed essentially for homogenous use, when in reality what happened is that we were able to form groups or silos based on our beliefs, values, and what matters most to us.

This is never truer than within an organization. Think about Facebook founder Mark Zuckerberg, who created a platform that would forever change our world. His initial desire, as the story goes, was simply to use Facebook as a way to pick up girls. He was able to attract and recruit other coders with the same values and beliefs and thus Facebook was born. Can you imagine what our world would be like without this social media platform? Advertisers, marketing gurus, companies who thought that Facebook was just a fad, realized the power this platform had in the way we communicate and reach our end users, clients, and customers. What we know is that there are groups or tribes that are already being formed and are in existence, and they are looking for a leader. The tribe has the same values or ideas, and they are waiting for someone who is willing to shift and challenge the status quo. The goal is simply to find the group that already has the yearning and desire that you have, and for you to show up and lead. This is the power of tribe-building.

LEVERAGING THE TRIBE TO RECRUIT

Once you have identified your tribe, also known as your ideal client profile or your ideal employee profile, the next step is to leverage your existing tribe, employees, and community to recruit new employees. There are many ways to attract rock star and superstar talent; however, the best way is by referral. The best strategy is to become a "Best Place to Work" and let your employees decide who gets to be part of your "winning" culture.

Can you imagine the loyalty that you would create by letting your employees know that they are responsible for creating, keeping, and maintaining the culture? The process should be very easy and simple to do. It would begin with your sharing, during the hiring process, how your company recruits for new talent. For example, you could say something like this, "In order to keep our culture amazing, we truly rely on our employees to refer great people to us. It is our belief that like attracts like and since you are AMAZING, you probably know others who have your similar values, skill set, and experience. Our hope is that you would refer these great people to our company, or if you stumble upon someone that you think would add value to our organization that you will refer them to us."

There are several companies that offer a referral bonus or incentive for their referrals. This is definitely something that you could introduce in your company. Typically, you will compensate the person after the individual makes it through the 90-day probationary period. Although this is a great incentive, I recommend that you get really clear about what motivates your employees. Everyone is not motivated by money and they would gladly *recommend* top talent just because they also want to *work* with top talent. If we look at what we talked about during previous chapters as to what motivates many people, it is the fact that they are part of a company that is making a difference and an impact. It is also important to know that people want to be able to grow, and this happens when they are surrounded by people who are playing at the top of their game.

CREATING YOUR WINNING CULTURE

The mistake that most companies make when creating a winning culture is the belief that all they need to do is focus on employees' perks, and by default they will have a great culture. Having a winning culture is not about giving your employees bonuses, days off, massages, etc. It is about rewarding your employees for performance and results.

Every company that I interviewed for this book had several things in common. The one thing that they ALL shared was the desire to have a great culture that focused on tracking and measuring their results. They were not just about having picnics and fun parties, but they measured their results and each organization was transparent about where the company was in regards to the goals set, accomplished, and achieved. What I also noted is that the goals were being measured daily and they were either placed on the wall where everyone could see or they had a visual scoreboard *(which is what Infusionsoft used)*. Each leader explained to me that the key word in having a winning culture was "winning."

Are you tracking the company's goals with your employees? Are you sharing the company's yearly, quarterly, monthly, or daily goals? If not, I would highly recommend that you start to implement this within your organization. People need to know where they stand and what part of the puzzle their roles play. As I stated earlier, you can't improve what you don't measure, and the first part of creating a winning culture is designing the spirit of competition within your organization. Here's the distinction of a Level 4 Culture—the competition is not between each other; the competition is normally the company vs. their competitors. With that said, I do recommend creating playful and light-hearted contests within each department which can spur comradery and fun in the workplace.

PROTECTING AND MANAGING YOUR TRIBE

Once you are clear what the vision, mission, guiding principles, and values of your organization are and you have clarity on the culture you desire to create, the next step is to protect and manage your tribe and company culture. Think of your tribe as a castle with a moat around it, and a drawbridge to allow those to go in and out. When you think about medieval times, especially when they were being attacked by their enemies, the sole goal was to get inside of the castle or to get the drawbridge down, so that they could take over the city. The army would normally be placed on the wall to prevent anyone from coming in who was not welcome. These people watched the city to make sure it was protected.

As you begin to build and design the culture that you desire, it is important that you first protect your tribe from outsiders or individuals who come to cause discord within your organization. This is similar to a bad apple that spoils the whole bunch. This is done by making sure that you hire and fire based on the mission, values, and guiding principles of the company, without exception. It is also important that during your employee orientation process that you institute a training specifically around your core values and company culture. Every employee is required to go through this training, from the CEO to the front line employees. By introducing this training, you bring clarity to the entire team and everyone knows what your company/organization stands for and what will and will not be tolerated.

Once you have this implemented, the next step is to hold the employees accountable to the core values, mission, and guiding principles of the organization. This can be done either formally or informally. I like to call it "catch the people who are doing it right." As a leader, if you see an employee living out your core values, you want to mention it to them openly, or acknowledge them in front of their peers or during company meetings. You also want to have a formal way of identifying if they are living out the core values during employee reviews.

Rewarding, recognizing, and coaching are essential in protecting and managing your tribe. As you start to recruit superstar and rock star employees, your company will be looked upon as one of the top places to work and, guess what? You will find that other companies will do their best to recruit and lure your employees to come work for them. My belief is that if you do right by your employees, all things being equal, they will always do right by you.

THE ENTITLEMENT TRAP

Here's the danger in building a winning culture—it's that sometimes you might experience what we call "the entitlement trap." Every company that was interviewed explained that there is a fine line between creating a "winning" culture and the danger of people feeling like they are entitled to employee perks, "just because." How do you know if your company has fallen prey to the entitlement trap?

Here's an example of an employee that I spoke to who very candidly shared this experience. This person was in the employees' dining room one day and noticed that they were out of the "hot fudge" for hot fudge sundaes that the employees liked to make. *(This company provides FREE food for their employees).* At that moment, the employee stated, "Wow, this place is really going downhill." That is when this employee thought, "What am I saying?" and became a victim of the entitlement trap.

It is so easy to do, especially as you are growing the company. You think that the way to win great talent is through all of the perks. Remember, that is not always the case. There were several companies that attached a perk with winning and achieving a certain goal or benchmark. One of the companies rewarded their employees with a pool table and foosball table for hitting one of their major goals. By creating your perks around achievement, not only will you connect the fact that you are building a "winning" culture, you will also connect that everything is not just given to the employees on a silver platter, but that there is a price to pay for having great perks.

The other challenge many companies will experience is when they have new employees who don't know what it is like *not* to have free lunches, massages, or company retreats, and the company hits a bad time and needs to remove some of the perks. At this time, you can see the entitlement trap show its ugly head and have people wanting to leave because we are no longer giving out chai tea.

Sounds crazy but I remember working for a company that literally spent $100,000 a year on herbal tea and when the recession hit, the organization made a decision to get rid of the herbal tea and exchange it for Lipton. Now, I grew up on Lipton so I was okay with it. I was just grateful that I had FREE tea but you would be surprised how many people were outraged because they no longer had herbal tea. When the CFO candidly shared that the cost of the tea was 2-3 people's salaries, it gave people perspective. Basically, the company had a decision to make, they could keep three employees or they could get rid of the herbal tea. Personally, I think they made the right choice. However, this is a great example of how the "entitlement trap" can show up in your company. How do you keep your company from falling into the entitlement trap? It is simply by giving people a realistic perspective and reminding new hires of the company's history. This is a great way to keep the employees grounded and grateful for all of their amazing benefits.

HIRE SLOW, FIRE FAST

I am often asked by my coaching clients and organizations that I train, how do you hire the right culture fit when you are in growth mode? My belief is that hiring the wrong fit will cost you in the end, so it is better to hire slow and fire fast. I had an opportunity to interview Reid Carr, CEO of Red Door Interactive, based out of San Diego. The strategy that Reid shared for hiring was absolutely brilliant; it is basically building your bench. Think about it—if you watch any sports, you have the first string that is on the field. They are your superstars and A-players, but they can be replaced by those who are on the bench. What Reid shared is that, for every position that his company has, he is actively recruiting up to two individuals as replacements. That way if he needs to hire someone, he is not scrambling to get just anyone in the position. Reid always has an A-player on the bench waiting to come in.

Can you do the same thing? Can you actively recruit at least 2-3 people to interview and have in the wings so you have them when you need them? The worst thing you can do is hire someone just because you have an immediate need. This could turn out to be a wrong culture fit that pollutes, contaminates, and destroys your company culture. It is worth the time to hire slow and make sure you have the right fit.

On the flip side, if you know that you have the wrong person within your organization, it is also important that you release her, as quickly as possible, back into the marketplace. Many employers have a hard time firing people because they understand that they are impacting someone's family and life. Yes, that may be true, but we also know that if you have someone in a position where she is not thriving, you can cause more damage to that person's esteem and keep her from actually finding the job or career that her talents are better suited for. The selfish thing is to keep someone who is not excelling and the more humane thing is to let this person go, to find a better job fit.

I recall working with a great CEO who had an amazing heart and was loyal to a fault. In the company there was a person who was in a position that was apparently the wrong fit, and for three years we would discuss why this person was in this role and how to get this person out. Finally, the CEO just got fed up and fired the employee. And guess what? The person went on to excel in another position for another company and the CEO now had the space to hire the right fit. The sad part is, this could have been done three years earlier, which would have kept both parties from the agony that they faced from having someone in the wrong role.

HIRING A FIT, NOT A PROJECT

This is also an example of hiring a project instead of a fit. How do I define a project? A project is someone who doesn't have the experience, skill set, or talent for the position that you are hiring for, but you have the belief that with the right training this person may do well. Now don't get me wrong, there are times when you will come across individuals who might not have the right experience or skill set but what they do have is discipline, tenacity, charisma, an ability to grasp and learn, and great potential. That's different. The project I am referring to is when you know someone who got let go, or a friend or a family member, and you are just trying to help them out because they need some money and you need a body in a position. I would strongly recommend not doing this. My rule of thumb is simply this, "Don't hire anyone that you are afraid to fire." That includes spouses, parents, siblings, and children.

When you hire someone as a favor or because you feel like you are helping him out, and he turns out not to be the right fit, you actually lose respect and credibility with your existing employees. As the leader, it is your responsibility to set the tone for the culture and your chief role, other being CEO or president, is to be "protector of the company culture." Everyone you hire is an example and representative of your company culture and more importantly your company's values. In the next chapter, we will examine exactly how to not only create actionable values, but how to align your values to create a winning entrepreneurial culture!

---

*"Outstanding leaders go out of their way to boost the self-esteem
of their personnel. If people believe in themselves,
it's amazing what they can accomplish."*

—*Sam Walton*

BRINGING IT ALIVE: ALIGNMENT CHALLENGE 5

Step Five: Never-ending Improvement *(The Power of Tribe-building)*

1. How can you introduce the power of tribe-building to your organization? What is the #1 constraint that is keeping your company from hiring, based on culture/ values above technical expertise?

    _____

    _____

    _____

2. Name some examples of how you can manage and protect your culture from the "Entitlement Trap."

    _____

    _____

    _____

3. Examine some ways that you can build a winning culture with your external customers *(i.e. vendors, clients, and employees' families)*.

    _____

    _____

    _____

New Business Culture Revealed: Case Studies from the "Best Companies to Work For" —Red Door Interactive

RMW: How would you define a winning culture?

Reid Carr *(CEO)*: Well, I think I really need to break this down—winning means successful, as in getting results. I think a lot of people tend to forget that when they think of culture. Know that it also needs to perform; a lot of people get out there and think that it has to be about having fun. And I think that it's about the dynamics of an environment that is healthy, productive, and enjoyable but which may not always be fun. It's not that the environment won't be fun, there are other things like tough projects, but in the end is a place where everyone is trying to get to a common and clearly defined end result.

I think a great culture is subjective and it will appeal to some and not others. Let me break it down to how we got to where we are. When I was writing the business plan for the company and recognized what it takes to be a large consultancy that is paid by the hour, I looked at other companies being paid by the hour and my question was, "Why are some folks getting paid $1,000 per hour while some charge $100 an hour?" And I recognized that it came down to people finding more value in that one person's hour than in the other's. Then it got down to, "How do you make sure your people across the board are the people that other people would be willing to pay the most for?"

So then I recognized that you really need to have great experience, education, training, and other things that would make them more valuable. I think part of the way we developed this rock star culture began with, "How do we make the most money?" And I think most people don't start there when they are creating their culture— they start with, "I want it to be fun."

I recognize, for example, what is commonly mistaken about a culture that is like ours and certainly other ad agencies, is that there are ping pong tables and foosball tables and stuff like that. So I made a conscious decision a long time ago that we wouldn't have any of that. We have social things here and there but that is not what's going to define our culture. I will give a specific example. I was working for an agency in L.A. that had a full course basketball court in the middle of our office and I remember one night we were playing an organized game, and the ball trickled into someone's work area, who picked that ball up and punted it. The person was so pissed that the ball rolled into that space—on some levels it was after hours, and I think it was fair and okay that we were playing basketball—but while we were having fun it was disrespecting someone who was trying to get work done and I recognized that if we have a ping pong table here and you are playing ping pong while someone else is on deadline and needs something from you, this person may feel mad and disrespected, and that's not fun.

RMW: That is interesting. I don't think I shared that I'm originally from Michigan and worked for BBDO, and I remember specifically when I worked in the creative department and eventually ended up working for the CFO. But when I worked in the creative department, it was a totally different dynamic. At that time we had about 1,500 employees, and they had a foosball table, a pool table, and they had the remote cars and all the other departments hated them. They wanted to know how a $10,000 pool table got approved. And they became territorial and would say, "This is our pool table and no one else can play." So I can see how that could become a challenge.

RC: That's not the goal to create icons like that. People forget that's a symbol. The pool table is a symbol and when you start having those icons, it creates the haves and have nots, instead of understanding that we are here to do great work for our clients and the icons are not our mission.

RMW: Speaking of mission—when you first started your business plan, did you have your mission statement all built out or fleshed out? At what point did you map that out?

RC: It's interesting. I have a different philosophy. We don't have a mission statement, and I thought about how people say you have to have mission, vision, and values so I sat down to work on that one time. Then I started thinking about what a mission is in a military sense, which is to accomplish an objective and be strategic over a certain amount of time, and I realized that we do that all day long. We didn't create this company to be the largest company doing X and being Y. That's not why I started this company, so we have a mission *(per se)* over a year where I would say this is what we want to do to get us to the next level, but it's not the 30-year mission statement with very audacious goals.

So we then created a purpose statement and that purpose is why we come to work each day. And that is what you will see on the wall: "Together we create to help each other win." And we got back down to why we show up each day, why we stay late, and at the end we break it down. Number 1 is together – together is better, we are all in this together. We create – why it's important that we state it this way is because as consultants we are not always creating stuff. We actually want to build things. It's interesting how it shapes what we do, especially with our clients who continually want ideas *(that's no fun)*. It's deflating.

It's amazing how much time you can spend talking and not doing, and this is one of the reasons why I believe people leave companies *(my suspicion)* and that is not uncommon. To help each other –the other thing I recognized is that I play a part, but we can't do it on our own and we will deflect this back to our clients as well, so they have to help us, they have to approve our things, they have to give us direction and if they are not able to help us, help them, then it becomes very challenging. So we are in it together. And that has to happen internally, with the manager and the employees. We have a lot of deep conversations around "How can I help you win? What's your goal?" And to help each other, there is inherent accountability within that. To help you WIN – what's fun about a game if you are not able to win? So we look at "How are we getting there?" We look at goals, metrics, and numbers, which are not always fun.

How do you craft a culture? It is all about the behavior and therefore the purpose/mission statement and values should drive the decisions that you make.

The reasons why I chose a purpose statement was to make things inspiring so we will want get up and do this tomorrow. We are giving something and getting something, and if we recognize the gift that we are giving and someone else sees the value of that gift and says thank you, then we will want to do it again tomorrow.

RMW: So the purpose statement took the place of the traditional mission statement. At what point did you craft that? And did you do it by yourself or was it collective?

RC: It was collective. I don't think the time was as important as what was going on at the time. It was about four years ago and what I recognized was when you first start doing the business, you are the one doing the work, and then you bring some people onboard and you are just doing some of the work. Then you bring on managers and you have to manage the managers who are managing the people doing the work. And I think that is the juncture when you are managing the managers doing the work when I wanted to sit down and really create this. Values are inherent, not that I sat down and said these are my personal values, but you make decisions based on your background, your experiences, the values that you adopted whether they have been taught or are part of your life experiences.

Our purpose statement has been the purpose statement from the day we created it, but we originally had eight core values and now we only have five. And it's funny because our approach to it was very instructional—I didn't like the one-word values like "trust" because there are different interpretations of those based on experiences and backgrounds. So we wrote eight sentences and then a couple of years later when we were doing all of our reviews to make sure people are measured on the values and hired by the values, I had a suspicion that the people didn't remember the values. So I went to the management team at our planning meeting and I gave them a card and a pencil and I said, "Write down our values." I said that you are a manager and you are managing people around our values and when they sat down to do the exercise, they wrote maybe 3 or 4 and some of them were a mismatch and I said, "This isn't going to work." So we changed it back to the one-word values and the shift in it was being clear on the definition of the words.

It's interesting that there are some CEOs who personally hire every employee—that's not what I do at all. During the on-boarding when they arrive, I go through the values and I get to know each and every employee and talk to them specifically about how we define each word because there is a nuance to them that I want them to understand. Then I come back to meet with them 30 days later. This gives them the flexibility to make decisions based on the spirit of the values.

RMW: So the values are actually empowering them to make the decisions that are best for the organization.

RC: Exactly. I tell them that I spend my life to get out of work. If you have everything you need to make a decision, it eliminates the need to run it up the ladder. We hired you for a reason, you are good at what you do, and then there is the culture aspect of it, which is huge in empowering them to succeed.

RMW: So it sounds like you trust the people that you have

and they trust you. I've trained a lot of companies and organizations and you can tell they are trying to shift, but the issue is lack of trust. Trusting their employees to do the right thing …

RC: I think there is a presumption on those occasions where the boss, the CEO, or whomever it might be, is expected to always have the right answer. I think that is an incorrect presumption, because there are times when there might not *be* a RIGHT answer—it may just be the BEST answer—and it's not going to end up good. There are probably extenuating circumstances that you do not touch every single day, so you probably don't have all the information. Even if they are supposedly giving you the information, you still might not be getting it and the fact is too, I think the executives or whomever is making the decisions these days, would say we might as well figure it out as we go and if I make a few mistakes and if they make a few mistakes, we might as well work on it together.

RMW: It sounds like your company hires individuals based on values. What is the practical application of that? How do you go about it?

RC: At first it starts with the recruiting process. About a year ago when we did the measurement, we found out that 100% of our new hires were brought in by one of our employees. That's when we realized that birds of a feather flock together. So if you've got good employees, they know other good employees.

Everyone in the whole company is responsible for recruiting, so we are very clear on what we are in need of and what we are looking for. But also that we are always recruiting for every position.

RMW: Is there an incentive?

RC: Yes, we give an incentive as well. We decided to do it, and initially I was opposed because I didn't want money to be the incentive. I wanted them bringing good people because they want to work with good people. So we decided to just balance them both. The biggest part of that is always recruiting for every position, and we have a least three candidates all the way through the process. And what I mean by process is, we start with career history, we do a phone screen, a focus interview *(there are four people who do four different interviews based on values specifically)*, and that includes core areas of the role they will be involved in. Then there is an in-depth interview *(which goes through the entire work history and includes references)*. We determine who we want to talk to from their references.

So it goes back to the fact that we are always recruiting, and it relates back to our culture because we ask our best clients, our best vendors, and our best people specifically *(we have a script for this, "Now that you know a little about us, who we stand for, and who we are, who is the best (blank)/*job title *that you ever worked with that you think would be a great fit for us?"* What we have heard in the past is, "What are you recruiting for, and what position you have open?" They may say they know this person from the past but they don't know if they are looking. That's not the point. I just want to meet people who are like us, who are the best that you know, because if it's not them, then it is someone they know. And so we are always doing this, and if they are willing to be part of something like this and, even if they are not actively looking, consider us as a viable Plan B. And if they are smart they absolutely do that, and if they don't they probably are not a great fit.

But the point is, you're never going to know what might happen. Why not talk to us and at some point, if something changes, you have us in your back pocket? Hey, we take you through all of the interview stuff on your own time during a certain time period *(it could be two years)*, whatever is convenient and at this point, so we are like, "Hey, you know what? We have this position open that we will send to you via email, and if you don't want to take it or if something changes for you, let us know and then we will email you if we have another opportunity or foresee we might have an opportunity, then we will take you up on it.

So within that, we are not hiring in desperation, we have people who have been through the process and they have been brought in by people who know us and that's how it works.

RMW: Amazing. You know that you are not hiring in desperation, especially when you find companies that are in a growth spurt. So how do you protect your culture? I had the opportunity to interview a lot of great companies with great cultures, and sometimes this sense of entitlement seems to creep in. Have you ever experienced that and how do you protect yourself?

RC: When you think about entitlement, it is wanting something for nothing. You want something, but what are you willing to give for it, because you have to understand the economics of a business. There's money coming in and money going out, you are either going to bring money in or you are going to take money out. As it stands right now, this paycheck is money going out and how are you going to create ways to generate money coming in? There are not many ways to do that...you can generate more business or you do work and do it more effectively. We do reviews and it's interesting, we have had people who told us that they never had a review or they were supposed to have a review but it didn't happen. One of the questions we ask when we are interviewing people is, "How were you rated on your last review?" And they might say, "Well it's supposed be every year but I only had one in seven years." We do it the other way—we do four every year. Each one is different than the others, but they are very in-depth. We are very public and we have fun.

Chapter Eight

HOW TO BECOME A LEADER THAT OTHERS WILL FOLLOW

"Leaders aren't born, they are made. They are made by hard effort, which is the price which all of us must pay to achieve any goal which is worthwhile."

– Vince Lombardi

As I mentioned, the goal is not just to attract great talent, it is also to develop great talent. How do you train the new generation or emerging leaders to maintain and protect the entrepreneurial culture of your organization? It starts by understanding the best way to lead, as well as shattering the old paradigm, including leadership styles that create a culture of fear versus a culture that is collaborative and innovative.

One of my favorite quotes is from *Spiderman* when his Uncle Ben tells Peter Parker, "With great power comes great responsibility." The challenge that our new generation and emerging leaders are facing is that they have never been in this position before and they sometimes model leadership styles that are no longer effective in the new corporate paradigm.

FIVE TYPES OF BAD LEADERSHIP STYLES

Let me share some examples of leadership styles that will not only destroy your culture, but will result in your best people leaving the organization if left unchecked:

The Compulsive Leader

Compulsive leaders feel like they have to do everything themselves. They try to manage every aspect of their business, often refusing to delegate, and cannot resist having their say on everything. As they lack trust in others, they cannot let anyone else take responsibility; therefore they restrict personal growth in their teams.

Compulsive leaders have many other traits. They are perfectionists who must follow highly rigid and systematized daily routines, and are concerned with status. Thus they strive to impress their superiors with their diligence and efficiency, and continually look for reassurance and approval. These types of leaders can oftentimes become workaholics, and their teams may be viewed as failing if they don't keep pace. Spontaneity is not encouraged within the team, as it bucks the routine.

The sad part about the compulsive leader is, despite their appearance of total control, such leaders can be ripe to explode on the inside. Their attempts to keep control are linked to their attempts to suppress anger and resentment, which makes them susceptible to outbursts of temper if they perceive they are losing their grip.

The Narcissistic Leader

Narcissistic leaders are focused on themselves. Life and the world revolve around them, and they must be at the center of all that is happening. Whilst they exaggerate their own merits, they will try to ignore the merits of others, or seek to devalue them, because other people's accomplishments are seen as a threat to their own standing. The worst type of narcissistic leader cannot tolerate even a hint of criticism and disagreement.

Where possible, they will attempt to use the merits of others for their own advancement, and think nothing of stepping on people to get ahead. Their own feeling of self-importance means they are unable to empathize with those on their team because they cannot feel any connection.

Some narcissistic leaders take on a sidekick *(also known as the Yes man/woman)*, but this person is expected to toe the line at all times and serves only to reflect praise onto their leader, and to loudly approve all that they do.

The Paranoid Leader

Paranoid leaders are exactly as they sound—paranoid that other people are better than they are—and so they view even the mildest criticism as devastating and a huge attack on their character. They are liable to overreact if they sense they are being attacked, especially in front of other people. This can manifest itself in open hostility.

This attitude is the result of an inferiority complex that perceives even the most constructive criticism in the wrong way. The paranoid leader will be guarded in his dealings with other people because he does not want to reveal too much of himself in case his weaknesses are attacked or undermined. These leaders may be scared that their position is undeserved, and therefore can be deeply suspicious of colleagues who may steal their limelight or perhaps challenge their position.

This is not always a wholly negative trait. A healthy dose of paranoia can be a key to success in any business, because it helps to keep the leaders on their toes, always aware of opportunities that should not be missed. It is the opposite end of the spectrum to being complacent, and can make for a very successful venture.

The Co-dependent Leader

Co-dependent leaders do not enjoy taking the lead, and instead seek to copy what others have done or are doing. They avoid confrontation and would rather cover up problems than face them head-on. Planning ahead is not their forte. They tend instead to react to whatever comes their way, rather than acting to alter outcomes or achieve goals.

Co-dependent leaders, therefore, are not leaders at all. They are reactionary and have the habit of keeping important information to themselves because they are not prepared to act upon it. This can clearly lead to poor outcomes because all the pertinent facts are not known to those below the leader, who may be charged with making decisions. It is not unlikely that such leaders would be perceived as workaholics, for they normally wouldn't take vacations or days off for fear of being found out.

This type of leader avoids confrontation and is thus liable to accept a greater workload, rather than respond negatively to any request. They are prone to be people pleasers and will accept the blame for situations they have not caused.

The Passive-Aggressive Leader

Passive-aggressive leaders feel like they need to control everything and when they can't, they cause problems for those who are in control. However, they are sneaky in their ploys and are very difficult to catch. Their main characteristics are that they can be stubborn, purposely forgetful, intentionally inefficient, complaining *(behind closed doors)*, and they are also known to be procrastinators.

Typically, if they feel they are not firmly in the driving seat, they will jump out and puncture the tires when no one is looking, then fake horror and pretend to search around for a tire iron.

This type of leader has two speeds: full speed ahead and stopped. When situations do not go their way, they will offer their full support for whatever has been decided, then resort to gossip and back-stabbing, willfully causing delays and generally creating upset. When confronted, they claim to have been misinterpreted. Passive-aggressive leaders are often chronically late for appointments, using any excuse to dominate and regain control of the situation.

Dealing with passive-aggressive leaders is a draining and frustrating effort that will sap all of your energy. They are not averse to short outbursts of anger to regain some control, but are ultimately fearful of success since it leads to higher expectations. They have a deep fear of making a mistake and being perceived as wrong.

You may have experienced these five leadership styles during your career, and if you were to think back and reflect, you will probably agree that some of these leaders may have gotten results, but at what cost? An example of a bad leadership style is when I worked for a large advertising agency and Chrysler was a major client. At the time I worked for them, they actually had three advertising agencies and when they merged with Daimler, the new management asked the question, "Why do we need three advertising agencies?" They decided that they would have all three companies bid for the account.

The company that I worked for was elated because they felt like they were the best company for the job and, as a matter of fact, this company had worked with Chrysler during the time when Lee Iacocca was in charge. We felt like we had the upper hand because when Chrysler was struggling back in the 70's, this company worked for them pro bono for three years until they got back on their feet. Surely they would be loyal. Well, not so.

It turned out that we lost the account not because the other agency was better than us, but it was simply a cost decision. They were cheaper than us. We then learned that 1,500 people would be let go a week before the Thanksgiving holiday. The advertising agency that won the business then made a very strategic move. They hired 500 of the best employees from my ad agency, including the CEO of the company and me!

Now the challenge that the new company had was how to merge the two cultures and how to make the transition smooth. Each new person who was brought in had to go through the hiring process, including being interviewed by their new manager/supervisor. I share this story because I remember the interview as if it was yesterday. The person I was reporting to was named Helen and she resented the fact that I was coming on board *(after all, for years my company was the enemy of hers)*. The interview, I was told, was just a formality—I was already a shoe-in because of my former boss who was the CFO of the old agency and was good friends with the CFO of the new company.

I recalled when I met with Helen that she shared with me that she understood that I was going to school to get my degree and asked how I saw myself advancing in the future. Before I could open my mouth she replied, "Nowhere!" She went on to say the "only position you could advance to is mine and I'm not going anywhere."

This was the beginning of my short-term relationship with the new company. I lasted a total of six months before I left to find a company that respected and valued both my talents and gifts, and that would celebrate and challenge me to grow. Helen was my real world example of the leader I did not want to be.

HOW TO LEAD AND INFLUENCE PEOPLE

As you begin to train the new generation of leaders, it is important for them to understand that leading people has nothing to do with managing them. Too many managers are trying to micromanage their staffs, all the while forgetting to lead them effectively.

If you want to become a strong leader and if you want to raise up strong leaders, it begins with leading by example. This means you have to show your team that you walk your talk. By doing so, you will earn their respect and create a lifelong tribe member who will move mountains to please you. Do not become a manager who hides behind the office door while commanding your staff. This is not going to get you respect in the workplace and can create a Level 2 Culture.

Ultimately, the success of any organization lies in the hands of its employees and NOT the managers. Think about it. A manager's responsibility is to organize and manage business systems, systems that will see to the finalization of projects.

If your staff is unhappy, it will soon show in their lack of productivity. This will influence your bottom line. Chances are, customer complaints will start to amass and office gossip will run hot. This is counterproductive to running a well-oiled machine.

As you begin the process of training your new emerging leaders, you must transfer your authority and empower them to step into the role of leadership.

CHANGING MINDSETS BY EMPOWERING OTHERS

A great leader must take responsibility for her team's performance, which means leaders must be happy that the direction of the team is one which the leaders thinks is best. Although it is useful to have creative sessions with team members to bat around a few ideas, the overarching goals that the team must fulfill are most often set by the leader or an authority above the leader.

The challenge is, therefore, to get the team "onside" with the given aims, even when some team members may wholeheartedly disagree with them or even balk at the idea that these have been imposed on them from above. Let me just say that if you have a Level 3 or 4 Culture, you will probably not experience this reaction. However, if your culture is at Level 1 or 2, more than likely you will get resistance.

Despite the accepted hierarchy of any workplace, for a team to work most efficiently, its members – especially higher level ones – may want to feel they are contributing more than spade work; they may like to feel that they have chosen where some of the plots should be dug. This presents a challenge for the leader who cannot just let his or her subordinates have free rein. The team must be made to feel involved and motivated. Or perhaps the situation is worse, and the team is beginning to show a little disobedience. How then to provoke a positive response in them?

The answer is by empowering your team, as far as possible. Short of handing over the reins and heading home, the motivational leader must be able to create a sense that the team is actively involved in the process and contributing in a real sense to the overall outcome of the project. This can involve learning how to make your suggestions appeal to them. This may mean you solicit their opinions and take their best ideas on board. Or you may have shown them how your goals are shared and that their futures are tied to the overall success of the organization. It may be as simple as connecting the dots of how their job performance is creating a better lifestyle for them and their families.

Empowering others does not just mean employing tactics that persuade other people to embrace your own opinion or goals. It can also mean demonstrating leadership qualities that inspire others to act at their very best, no matter what is asked of them. Such leadership qualities would be most in evidence in the armed services, where the end result of potentially being killed is rarely going to elicit a whoop and a cheer. Soldiers are empowered to greatness by the examples set by their commanding officers.

Sometimes, it is just a matter of being an admirable and inspirational human being. Of course, some are born with more of these qualities than others, but we can strive to lead by example, so that others will feel empowered to make great things happen. If you think about the great leaders that you have come in contact with, what are the qualities, characteristics, and traits that you most admired about them? Take a minute and write them down. The interesting thing is, those qualities are just a reflection of the qualities that you possess. Understand that they are just a reflection of the true you.

When I am brought in by a company to train their new managers or leaders, or when I am hosting one of my live Emerging Leaders Workshops ™ I always ask the same question, "Why are you here?" Since the majority of the attendees are there voluntarily, I am curious to know what they are looking to get out of our time together. The answer is always the same, "I want to be a better leader." I am assuming that if you picked up this book, you too have a strong desire to be the best leader possible and you want to help others to be the best leaders they can be.

TEN WAYS TO BE A BETTER LEADER

1. **Ask to be judged.**

   Finding out what others think of your leadership skills can really help you change for the better. Sometimes leaders can be so wrapped up in appraising others, that they do not seek appraisal from below, only from their own superiors. This is why the 360° feedback is so powerful. Your team is the best source of feedback, because they are on the receiving end of your "skills" every day. Honesty should be encouraged, but bear in mind that it may only be anonymous feedback that holds the truth if your team believes you are going to use it against them or become defensive about what they say. If you have created a trusting and open environment, this should not be a problem.

2. **Don't abuse your power.**

   If people are questioning why certain things are done, or the logic of decisions, never pull rank in response. *(I hate it when someone responds "because I said so.")* Your team should feel empowered, if only by your taking the time to explain the rationale for any decisions that you have made. Your team must be on your side. This will not happen just by telling them that the decision is the right one because you are the boss. Your team may not agree, but they should know why a situation "is what it is."

3. **Believe your team is intelligent and can be trusted.**
    This should be obvious, especially if you hired the
    right fit and took your time to onboard them properly.
    Your team should be allowed to take actions and make
    decisions. As I stated earlier, trust is a vital component
    of leadership skills. If you can't trust people to do their
    jobs, then you have the wrong people, or you're not
    managing them properly.

    I love basketball and one of my fondest memories
    is watching a Miami Heat game *(when LeBron James
    was in the championship)* and the coach had them in a
    huddle, telling them repeatedly, "Do your job!" After
    they won the game, a reporter asked him about it and
    he stated that "These are some of the most talented
    players in world, and my job is to empower them to do
    what they do best."

    With that said, let your people do what they are there
    to do without having you peer over their shoulders
    every fifteen minutes, asking them what they are doing
    with their time. Let them do their jobs, so you can
    do yours.

4. **Listen.**
    Truly listening to your team is one of the greatest
    leadership skills. Good listeners come across as
    genuinely interested, empathetic, and concerned to

find out what's going on.

I remember Mary Kay Ash from Mary Kay Cosmetics, who shared a story of how she was so excited to win a sales award and attend a ceremony where she finally got to meet the CEO of the company that she was working for at the time. She shared how when she was introduced to the CEO, his eyes darted around and he barely said two words to her. It was because of her disappointment that she made a point of being fully present with the person she was speaking to. She understood that for many people it was their dream to connect with her and she didn't take her status for granted.

All great leaders have great communication skills. Unhappy team members can only exist where their problems have not been aired. Create an environment where problems can be discussed so that solutions can be found.

5. **Stop being an expert on everything.**
   Leaders often achieve their positions by being proficient in a certain area, and will usually have an opinion on how to fix problems. They believe it's better to tell someone what to do, or even to do it themselves, than give their team the opportunity to develop their own solutions, and therefore exercise their creativity.

6. **Be constructive.**
    Negativity breeds negativity and contempt. How you communicate has a profound effect on your team, as a whole and individually. Criticisms will always need to be made by leaders, but try to make them constructive and deliver them without emotional attachment.

7. **Judge your success by your team's.**
    The true success of a leader can be measured by the success of the people who work for them. You cannot be a successful leader of a failing team, just as you cannot be a successful general of a defeated army. Your focus should always be on building your team's skills and removing the obstacles in their way.

8. **Don't be a narcissist.**
    I shared earlier the five bad leadership styles and this one is worth repeating. Nothing is more annoying for team members than leaders who make their decisions based on how good it will make them appear to their superiors. A key leadership skill is integrity. Integrity is about doing the right thing, and allowing praise where praise is due, even if that is not at your door.

9. **Have a sense of humor.**

   People work better when they are enjoying themselves. The work itself may be dull, but the environment does not have to be. Stifling fun also means stifling creativity. It is no surprise that every company that I interview includes "fun" either in their core values or as part of their culture experience. Team members love it when the leader joins in and has fun. This does not have to create a flippant atmosphere; on the contrary, it actually is an essential ingredient to team building.

10. **Don't be too distant.**

    It is possible for leaders to show a more human side, without revealing their innermost secrets. If mutual respect exists, this should not be seen as vulnerability, but rather a sign that you are a human being, just like your team members are. Only when your team gets to know the real you, will the true foundations of good leadership— trust and respect— be properly established.

"You don't lead by hitting people over the head—
that's assault, not leadership."

— *Dwight Eisenhower*

Chapter Nine

GROOMING THE NEXT GENERATION OF LEADERS

"As a leader, your role is to present the stage,
not become the performer."

– Linda Hill

HOW TO IDENTIFY YOUR RISING STARS

This is a question I am frequently asked while training organizations on how to attract, develop, and keep their top talent: "How do you know a rising star from a falling star?" It is, first and foremost, by getting clear and identifying what you value most in your employees.

What are the characteristics and traits of those whom you might deem to be the rock star employees? Is it being a self-starter? Or maybe you value creativity and innovation? Does this person have a natural propensity to problem-solve issues or bring you solutions when things are off-track?

The goal of your organization is to become a place where others want to work. I love the philosophy of Reed Hastings, CEO of Netflix, who actively views his culture as a sports team. His job is to hire a coach *(manager)* whose focus is to bring out the best from each employee. If you desire to be the best in your industry *(similar to a sporting team)*, you want to recruit and draft the top talent, and that happens by winning.

Consider this. No one wants to be on a losing team. As a matter of fact, most of the companies that were interviewed for this book shared that they focused on stacking their benches with the best talent. People want to work with those who are the best, because they challenge them to become better.

By creating an environment of growth and learning, you will begin to see the rising stars rise and once you identify who they are, your next step is to give them an opportunity to grow and expand. This is through an organized process, or by giving them more duties and tasks that will develop their talents and leadership abilities.

MENTORING THEM TO LEAD

In Sheryl Sandberg's book *Lean In*, she shares about the lack of women in leadership roles, and how many women do not step up or lean in to new executive level positions because they feel that they have to choose between having a successful career and raising a family.

There are many women who desire to have more access to mentorship within their organizations but don't know where to begin. When seeking to groom the next generation of leaders, your organization's coaching and mentoring must become a priority as you engage and develop your merging leaders.

Nevertheless, there are more and more women seeking to become leaders within their organizations, so this is not solely a conversation that is specific to gender. Although, when you examine the vast amount of employees exiting the corporate space, you can attribute a large percentage of women who flee the workforce because of their desire for flexibility and work/life balance. Millennials are no exception. They are also looking for leaders who are willing to invest in their future and mentor them as they move into leadership roles.

So does your company have a leadership development mentoring program in place? If not, what are some things that you can do to introduce such a program within your organization?

As we consider grooming the next generation of leaders, the other bigger concern is how to transfer the knowledge and expertise from the Baby Boomers to the next generation. There are a number of corporations that, anticipating the drain of technical knowledge and expertise caused by the departure of Baby Boomers, have chosen to implement programs designed to impart the valuable knowledge these employees possess. Some examples of companies that are proactively preparing for the transition of the Baby Boomers are:

- **Lockheed Martin Space Systems** – Anticipating the experience and technological shortfall to come, Lockheed created a Critical Skills Management Program which pairs older experts with junior employees to mentor them and increase their knowledge to the expert level.

- **Duke Energy** – The North Carolina utility giant has developed a software tool that digitizes the results of interview sessions with senior engineers for use in training. The program has helped accelerate the learning curve for younger employees.

- **Wells Fargo** – The banking conglomerate has devised a master's-level certification program that pairs young professionals with their "Boomers Connection" network members, for a mutually beneficial collaboration that awards MA certification in connection with a major Minnesota university.

- **Yoh** – Staffing agency Yoh supplies temporary staff from a pool of older workers with specialized knowledge in a number of industries. These seasoned workers accept part or full-time positions for project-to-project or contingency assignments.

- **Staff Management/ SMX** – This agency manages a pool of retirees with recreational vehicles who fill in when needed to supplement their retirement income. They plan extended vacations around job bridge assignments.

MAKING THE TRANSFER

Mentoring can be beneficial to both generations, but each generation must make the effort to understand the other. Younger employees need to appreciate the value that experience can impart, then willingly accept that knowledge and put it into practice. Older workers will need to have the patience to teach the younger generation their strict work ethic and the techniques they have used to help build a business into a successful enterprise. By meeting in the middle, both generations stand to gain in the continuation of the growth of the business and in leaving a legacy of success.

CREATE OPPORTUNITY FOR GROWTH

As discussed in previous chapters, one of the top reasons why people quit their jobs is because they do not have an opportunity to grow. This is something that I want to reiterate because of the weight that it has on attracting, developing, and keeping your top talent.

Many companies are under the assumption that they have to promote someone to a position with a title in order for them to stay. That is not necessarily true. Great employees want the opportunity for expansion and this can be done without giving them a title or even more money.

Some ways that you can create an environment for growth are:
- Cross-training
- Giving more responsibility
- Empowering them to make decisions that are in alignment with the company goals and objectives
- Giving them an opportunity to do training

These are some ways that you can ignite a spirit of growth within your organization.

One of Google's famous perks is the "20 percent time program." Google allows its employees to use up to 20 percent of their work week at Google to pursue special projects. That means for every standard work week, employees can take a full day to work on a project unrelated to their normal workload. Google claims that many of their products in Google Labs started out as pet projects in the 20 percent time program. Not only does this create an opportunity to grow within the organization, it also supports creativity and innovation, and stops boredom from creeping in.

PROVIDE A SAFE SPACE TO FAIL

Another common trait among those listed on the "Best Places to Work" is their philosophy around failure. Many of the top CEOs, including Steve Jobs, believed that if you are not failing, then you are missing the mark and you are playing it too safe.

In this fast growing and ever changing environment, the companies that will dominate are those who take on the spirit of the entrepreneur and are willing to fail forward. By letting your employees know that failing is part of the process and as long as they come to you quickly when mistakes are made, they will see that the culture accepts failure as part of the process and they are safe to do so.

It is important that, as you are grooming your emerging leaders, you have regular meetings *(i.e. 5-minute check-ins)* where you are able to mentor, coach, and support employees on this journey. This is not micromanaging. This is empowering them by letting them know that you are there to support them and if an issue arises, they can feel comfortable coming to you to share what's happening.

Many employees who work at a Level 1 or 2 Culture would either pass blame or hide the event in order to prevent retribution or fear of being fired. If you are working to have a Level 3 or 4 "winning" Culture, then you will encourage them to share their mistakes, for they are simply learning opportunities for the organization. And as they step into the role as leaders they are able to instill this same strategy in those who report under them.

All innovation happens because someone did not like the way something was being done, and set out to build a better mousetrap. Always remember that with innovation comes risk, and many times failure. It is all part of the process and should be rewarded and not hindered.

"Culture eats strategy for lunch. – Peter Drucker

Chapter Ten

ALIGN YOUR VALUES FOR IMPACT

"It is important for employees to see the company's
values as a reflection of their own.
Values are at the core of the social contract between
company and employee."
– Wichian Mektrakarn, CEO, AIS

KNOWING YOUR CORE VALUES, MISSION, AND PURPOSE

Every company that I interviewed expressed that the sole reason why they had a winning entrepreneurial culture came down to the fact that they had a clearly defined mission, purpose, or set of guiding principles, as well as actionable core values. What I have experienced over the years, both as an employee and as a trainer, is that most companies have a mission or purpose statement and most companies have values or guiding principles that the organization stands on. The challenge is that many company leaders do not know what their mission and vision and core values are, and therefore their employees also do not know what they are.

It is not enough just to have them—they must be your true north, and they are used to determine who you will hire and fire. Your values are also used to help you to stay the course and make decisions that are in alignment with what you state the mission, vision, and values of your organizations to be.

One of the mistakes that I see many companies make is they hire someone like me to help them get clear and focused on this concept, and then the amazing work they crafted is placed in a binder or on their website, never to be visited again *(until someone like me shows up again during transitions, mergers, or poor retention and high turnovers)*. Don't let this be you.

Another caveat to mention is that your mission or values should never be painted on your companies' walls or placed on the back of the employees' badges unless you have every intention to live, breathe, and abide by them on a daily basis.

Let's take a look at the core values of some of the companies I've interviewed, to give you a few examples and get you started:

Zappos' 10 Core Values
Deliver WOW through Service
Embrace and Drive Change
Create Fun and A Little Weirdness
Be Adventurous, Creative, and Open-minded
Pursue Growth and Learning
Build Open & Honest Relationships with Communication
Build a Positive Team and Family Spirit
Do More With Less
Be Passionate and Determined
Be Humble

Red Door Interactive Core Values
Inspire
Share
Evolve
Exceed
100% Jerk Free *(love this one)*

Intuit Core Values
Integrity without compromise
We care and give back
Be bold
Be passionate
Be decisive
Learn Fast
Win Together
Deliver awesome

Infusionsoft Core Values

We empower entrepreneurs

We listen, we care, we serve

We do what we say we'll do

We practice open, real communication

We face challenges with optimism

We check our egos at the door

We innovate and constantly improve

We do the right thing

We believe in people and their dreams

As you can see by the examples, these values are something that you can measure, track, and hold the individuals within your company accountable to. You are able to catch people living them, or not, which is the beautiful thing around making them actionable.

YOUR TURN

Now take a moment and examine your company's core values and ask yourself the question, "Are we living them daily?" If not, what shift can you make to bring them to life? Is it time for a re-do? If your company doesn't have an established written mission statement and core values, can you see why you may not be attracting the right employees to your organization?

Here's the beautiful thing about taking the time and crafting your values—once completed, you really will find that they are the magnet that is used alongside your winning entrepreneurial culture to attract superstars and top talent.

If you need help through this process, there is additional support located at www.TheCorporateExodusBook.com. If you would like for me to come to your organization to help you through the process, I invite you to reach out to us directly at contact@corporatecultureacademy.com.

WHY ARE YOU IN BUSINESS?

This is a question that every organization must answer, big or small. What is the reason for your existence? Why or how are you making this world a better place? One of my favorite books is *Start With Why* by Simon Sinek. In his book Simon shares that people do not care about *what* or *how you* do, as much as why you do it. The mission for Zappos, for example, is to deliver the best customer service possible. It has nothing to do with selling shoes and accessories, and if you had a deeper conversation with Tony Hsieh, you would learn that at his core, he just wants to deliver happiness. That is why he does what he does.

So why are you in business? What is your core motivation and the passion that wakes you up every morning? As you are better able to communicate this clearly in your business, it will become your messaging to recruit and keep top talent and develop your emerging leaders. Your reason for being in business will become your calling card, it will be the message you share on the megaphone or the microphone, on a stage, in a boardroom, or networking at a professional association.

Take a moment and answer this question, "Would the world miss your company if you didn't exist?" or another way to ask it is, "Would your customers, clients, or employees miss your company if you didn't exist?" This is a powerful question and if you answer "I don't know" or "No," it just shows that there is work still to do.

How would you need to show up differently in the marketplace to make yourself invaluable to your customers, clients, shareholders, and vendors? If you examine any of the companies listed as the "Best Places to Work," none of them started out with wanting to make a boatload of money. They all started off with wanting to make a difference in the lives of the people they are called to serve. Making a boatload of money and creating a huge following and fan base became their byproducts. And also in the process they are changing the way we do and look at business.

YOUR TRUE NORTH

Now that you have clarity around your mission, your values, and why you are in business, I would like you to think about what your *true north* is as a leader. What I've learned through my countless interviews and research is that every person who is doing great work knows where they are going. It doesn't mean that they are always on course—as a matter of fact, many times they will find themselves off the beaten path. It is easy to get distracted by the noise in the marketplace, and find yourself launching a new program or service that is out of alignment with what you are supposed to be doing. This is the value of knowing what true north looks like for you and your organization.

I can't tell you how many times I have worked with a CEO or executive who has reached their coveted goals, only to take a step back and ask, "Is this all?" There is a big difference between being fulfilled and achievement. Achievement satisfies the ego, where fulfillment satisfies the soul. I know you may be thinking, "Hey I thought this was a business book, how did we get onto this topic?" Simply stated, when you look at the emerging leaders and the next generation, the statistics are crystal clear. These individuals want to work for companies that have a "heart" and are making a difference.

If you want to stay on the leading edge and attract the best talent in the world, you must have a real conversation about the purpose and heart of your organization, and even more importantly, the purpose and heart of your leaders. The new corporate paradigm demands authenticity, honesty, and transparency, and understanding that folks can see behind the smoke and mirrors. While the new generation is not asking for leaders to be perfect, they are demanding that they be real.

Knowing your true north will come in handy when you find yourself lost. It is a matter of taking out the compass or the GPS and asking, "Where am I, and which way should I be going?"

ENGAGING YOUR TRIBE TO CREATE YOUR VALUES

I am aware that some of the readers of this book may be at a stage in their business where they do not have a mission and vision statement or core values. If that is you, don't beat yourself up. Many of the companies that I've interviewed were in business over ten years before they decided to take the time to create the written mission and vision statement and clearly define their values and principles. If you are at this stage and have employees, the beautiful thing is that they can help you craft your values. It is a simple process:

Step 1: Jot down ten values that are important to you.

Step 2: Ask your employees to list their top ten values.

Step 3: Compile a single list of all the values and ask them to pick their top ten.

Step 4: Have a town hall meeting and discuss them in terms of how they would look if they were actionable. Brainstorm examples.

Step 5: Take a vote.

Step 6: Announce the winners and then begin the process of incorporating them on a daily basis.

This is the beginning of something magnificent, but it requires that you commit to aligning your company values in order to build a winning entrepreneurial culture.

SCALING THE CULTURE FOR GROWTH

Once you have your values, you will be able to hire, fire, and review your employees based on the company's values, mission, and vision. However, what happens when you are in growth mode? How do you protect and keep your culture when you are growing or perhaps your organization is part of a merger or acquisition?

These are all important questions that you must consider when building a winning culture. How do you scale your culture for growth? The answer requires that you have clear values, mission, and vision. It is your value system that will allow you to support the culture as you grow your organization.

If you are serious about really committing to building your culture to attract and keep your top talent, then one of the things that you want to consider is having a values training period during the onboarding of your employees. This could be a one-day, multi-day, or two-week training where you go through the following:

- Why You Are In Business
- The Mission and Vision of the Company
- What You Believe
- Your Core Values and Guiding Principles
- The Company's Goals/Objectives

This is also a great opportunity for the CEO or leadership team to come in and speak with the new hires if possible. By doing this, you are setting the foundation for the employee to hear directly from their leaders what is important and why they are a valuable part of bringing the mission to life.

Living the company's values is the responsibility of every employee, and it begins with the leader and works throughout the entire organization. One other suggestion would be to create a Culture Ambassador Committee whose primary focus is to make sure that the company stays in alignment with their values, mission, and vision. The Culture Ambassador Committee could also discuss ways to build the team and culture through team building events and exercises.

It is your company's values that make your organization strong. Those companies researched and interviewed stated, without question or doubt, that their ability to scale and keep their dynamic culture is based on their values. More importantly, these companies make sure that every decision that is made on a daily basis is acted on based on their organizations' values, mission, and vision.

Ready...Set...GO!!

During these chapters I was able to share briefly some of the highlights of my A.L.I.G.N. system, which I use with top organizations in order to help them to create, build, and retain a winning culture, as well as to help them effectively develop their next generation and emerging leaders.

Just to recap, the A.L.I.G.N. system focuses on five key areas and takes a GPS approach to leadership development. This is your compass to make sure your company is going in the right direction. Some of the topics covered are:

1) Authentic Leadership Skills – This is where you examine the inner game of leadership. It involves building trust, respect, rapport, confidence, effective communication, and more.

2) Leveraging Talents & Gifts – How to coach for high performance, assigning people to the right tasks, team building, and leading a multi-generational workforce.

3) Innovation and Collaboration – How to strategically collaborate between departments, how to create an environment for creativity, and how to effectively empower your team.

4) Goal-setting – How to establish individual and team goals in alignment with company goals, accountability and measuring return on investments, and creating recognition and rewards for achievement...one size does not fit all.

5) Next Generation Leadership – How to seek out, attract, and develop your emerging leaders, retain top talent, keep your competitors from poaching your people, and tips for making your company recession-proof.

Leading people can be one of the most rewarding things you've ever done if you do it right. Do it wrong and leadership can quickly become a nightmare you hope to wake up from sooner rather than later. It is my hope that you will take action and, if we can help, do not hesitate to reach out. Building a winning culture is simple but it is not easy. It requires that you first have a commitment, the right team, the right leader, and the right plan. I have given you the framework of my blueprint that has been used successfully to help organizations attract, retain, and develop their next generation of leaders.

I know that once applied, your organization will be on its way to a Level 4 Culture and it will look unrecognizable. Until we meet in person, I look forward to hearing about your company's success!

MY GIFT TO YOU

It is my goal to shatter the old paradigm of doing business as usual. I am committed to helping companies to develop leadership and coaching skills around their employees' strengths. We are experts at helping you to create and maintain a winning entrepreneurial culture, even through dramatic organizational changes such as mergers, acquisitions, or changes in management or leadership.

If you are interested in learning more about how Corporate Culture Academy can support you and your organization, I invite you to schedule your complimentary, no-obligation, needs discovery session *(a $497 value)* by visiting us at: www. corporatecultureacademy.com.

ACKNOWLEDGMENTS

There are so many people to thank for helping me get my work out into the world. I oftentimes say that writing a book is like delivering a baby, there were a lot of sleepless nights, brainstorming, research, and tremendous effort involved.

To my husband Gord Wildman, who has been my biggest supporter and who always challenges me to play bigger and to take courageous leaps, even when I'm afraid. Thank you for reminding me what this work is all about. I know that you have my back. I love you forever and a day.

To my children, Antoine and Christopher, you are the reason that I am committed to making this world a better place. My legacy to you both is to never stop dreaming, and always believe the impossible. The world will give you the demand you place on it…no more or no less.

To my siblings, Carey, Billy, and Karen, we may not always see eye to eye but as our parents would always say, we are family, which is the most important thing.

To the ah-mazing CEOs, C-Level Executives, and front line employees who graciously shared their insights, struggles, and victories, and why you are a "Best Place to Work." Special heartfelt thanks to Randy Hetrick, CEO of TRX Training, Clate Mask, Co-founder of Infusionsoft, Reid Carr, CEO of Red Door

Interactive, Tony Hsieh and the Zappos Family for allowing me to tour your facilities and showcase your brilliant way of doing business.

Also, special acknowledgment to my team, copyeditor, and Chris Mendoza for working his graphic magic. Thank you for making me look and sound good.

And last but not least, I want to thank God for being with me every step of the way and for blessing me to make a greater difference and impact in this world. I am eternally grateful that You have chosen me to do this work. I will never take my assignment for granted.

CPSIA information can be obtained at www.ICGtesting.com
Printed in the USA
BVOW02*0710230616

453096BV00001B/1/P

9 780615 861104